GRACE
IS NOT A
GET OUT OF
HELL FREE
CARD

GRACE
IS NOT A
GET OUT OF
HELL FREE
CARD

STEVE FOSS

CHARISMA
HOUSE

Scripture quotations marked NIV are from the Holy Bible, New International Version. Copyright © 1973, 1978, 1984, International Bible Society. Used by permission.

Cover design by Lisa Rae Cox
Design Director: Bill Johnson

Visit the author's website at www.upperroomdfw.com.

Library of Congress Cataloging-in-Publication Data:
An application to register this book for cataloging has been submitted to the Library of Congress.
International Standard Book Number: 978-1-62136-278-4
E-book ISBN: 978-1-62136-279-1

While the author has made every effort to provide accurate telephone numbers and Internet addresses at the time of publication, neither the publisher nor the author assumes any responsibility for errors or for changes that occur after publication.

First edition

13 14 15 16 17 — 9 8 7 6 5 4 3 2 1
Printed in the United States of America

I would like to dedicate this book to my amazing wife, Carrie. Rarely in life do you find such a person of character and strength. I remember when God first spoke to me about her even before we met. God said, "Your wife will be a gift from Me to you because I love you." That she has truly been. From the moment I got saved, I dedicated myself wholly to God and His purposes. I decided I wouldn't date but wait until God revealed to me my perfect wife. God in His faithfulness brought me Carrie. After well over twenty years I can truly say Carrie is the most amazing woman I have ever met.

CONTENTS

Chapter 1

THERE IS A BATTLE RAGING

CAN'T DO IT—IT'S just too hard!" Those words have been uttered over and over again by Christians of all ages. Many well-meaning, Bible-believing, committed Christians are so frustrated in their walks with God that they are ready to give up on living a godly, Christlike life, or they are willing to give in to defeat. They think it is impossible to live holy and stop repeating the same sinful behaviors.

Many of them have had supernatural experiences with God, yet those divine encounters never seem to solve their problems. They continue to struggle and have defeated, unproductive spiritual lives. In a desperate attempt to reconcile the conflict between what the Bible says God has for them and their experiences in life, they resort to giving excuses such as, "Maybe it's not God's will for me to be free of this," or "It's not God's timing yet," or "This must just be my 'thorn in the flesh.'" These individuals create every excuse under the sun to explain why they are not experiencing the supernatural power of God in their everyday lives—why they do not have all things that pertain to life and godliness.

Others simply walk in denial. They're always confessing scriptures and saying God has given them the victory, when in reality nothing ever changes. They read books, listen to tapes, go to conferences, and watch Christian TV but experience no real lasting transformation, only temporary emotional fixes that don't stand the test of time. You would think I was writing about a small, select group of people, but the sad reality is that many born-again believers are living their lives without God's daily supernatural provision that empowers them to overcome evil and the sin in their lives.

With the thousands of promises given in the Word to deal with every aspect of our lives, why is the church living so far below what we confess and believe? If we truly are Abraham's seed, why are our blessings so far and few between? Why are so many Christians bound by habitual sin? Why have so many preachers fallen? Why is the divorce rate in the church as high as it is in the world? Why are the vast majority of our Christian youth leaving the church within two years of their high school graduations? Why is the church so poor?

We have had a greater level of teaching available to us than any previous generation. Yet despite the fact that many Christians have received some level of breakthrough in their lives, most are still not experiencing all the blessings promised us under the Abrahamic covenant. We know that we are supposed to have access to God's power for our everyday lives, yet how do we tap into it? Are we going to spend the rest of our Christian lives pretending everything is OK, or are we ready to get a spiritual breakthrough?

Once again the time has come for God to open the

windows of heaven and pour out divine revelation. It is time for God's people to understand what grace is and how to access the fullness of its glorious provisions.

It's Not What You Think

The doctrine of grace is at the core of our Christian faith. Without it we would still be without hope and without God. Yet many people, including preachers, misunderstand what grace actually is. Many people think grace is basically a "get out of hell free" card. Although grace is the way to salvation, it is not a license to live without accountability. Many Christians believe that because we are "under grace" and not the law, we are free from the righteous requirements of the Scriptures. Nothing could be further from the truth.

> Grace doesn't release us from the responsibility to live godly. It *empowers* us to live godly.

Although we can never earn our access to God, the way grace has been understood and applied has given many an unholy license to engage in ungodly living. Because people have come to view grace as an excuse to avoid accountability for the sin in their lives, they feel no obligation to pursue righteousness and holiness. You can easily tell if people believe this way about grace. Simply start preaching about holiness, and they will inevitably say, "Don't preach that to me! We are under grace, not under the Law."

Too many Christians wrongly believe that grace releases them from the responsibility to live a godly life.

This is simply not true. Grace doesn't release us from the responsibility to live godly. It *empowers* us to live godly.

Grace is the most significant, powerful, awesome gift from God that mankind has ever received. It is the key to accessing the power we need for everything we will face in life. The problem is, grace isn't what most people think it is. The good news is that it's *better!*

Make Up Your Mind

In this book we are going to explore one of the greatest keys to your victory. You are going to discover God's plan and purpose for your life. You are going to discover how you can truly live in 100 percent victory 100 percent of the time.

You, however, are going to have to make up your mind that you want to change. You are going to have to decide that enough is enough, and *now* is the time for a breakthrough. Jesus said in Matthew 11:12, "And from the days of John the Baptist until now the kingdom of heaven suffers violence, and the violent take it by force."

There are many areas of breakthrough that you will never receive passively. You will have to press deep into the spirit realm and aggressively lay hold of them. Far too often, in America especially, we want a microwave God who will give us instant answers and understanding. Although God in His mercy may at times sovereignly reveal hidden mysteries, He far more often makes His secrets known to those who diligently and desperately seek Him. Just look at the following scriptures:

> But without faith it is impossible to please Him, for he who comes to God must believe that He is,

4

*and that He is a rewarder of those who diligently
seek Him.*

—HEBREWS 11:6,
emphasis added

So that you incline your ear to wisdom, and *apply
your heart* to understanding; yes, *if you cry out
for discernment,* and lift up your voice for understanding, if you *seek her as silver,* and *search for
her as for hidden treasures; then you will understand the fear of the Lord, and find the knowledge
of God.*

—PROVERBS 2:2–5,
emphasis added

But from there you will seek the LORD your God,
and you will find Him *if you seek Him with all your
heart and with all your soul.*

—DEUTERONOMY 4:29,
emphasis added

> God has given us access to a great
> inheritance, but He has placed requirements
> upon us to receive His promises.

As you can see from these verses, God is looking for
those who will seek and search for Him with a passion
for truth. Some may wrongly think that this is a bit of a
"works" doctrine and that I am saying we have to prove
ourselves to God or earn His favor. This is not at all
what I am saying. You can never be good enough or do
enough to earn God's favor. However, God still requires
us to seek after truth.

Jesus said in Luke 11:9–10, "So I say to you, ask, and it will be given to you; seek, and you will find; knock, and it will be opened to you. *For everyone who asks* receives, and *he who seeks* finds, and *to him who knocks* it will be opened" (emphasis added). God didn't create us to be puppets. He made us joint heirs—co-participants with His divine life and purpose. He has given us access to a great inheritance, but He has placed requirements upon us to receive His promises.

He said that we must confess that Jesus is Lord in order to be saved (Rom. 10:9). He said that when we pray, we must pray in Jesus's name (John 14:13–14). He said we must enter His gates with thanksgiving and His courts with praise (Ps. 100:4). He says we must have faith in order to please Him (Heb. 11:6). God has placed many requirements upon us that are *not* legalistic works but simply acts of obedience. One of these acts is that we must seek Him diligently if we want to understand the secrets of heaven.

Clear Your Mind

In preparation for you to receive a new spiritual break-through, you must be prepared to clear your mind of all preconceived thoughts and ideas about grace. Most of us come to God and His Word with our minds filled with certain concepts and doctrines. We have developed a preset way of filtering the Scriptures and the truths that are preached to us.

All of us have filters that everything we read and hear must pass through. These filters are developed over years by our previous beliefs, experiences, hurts, likes, dislikes, and so on. Sadly these filters are often the greatest barriers to our receiving what God is trying to say to us.

We have seen this play out many times in recent decades. When the early teachers in the faith and prosperity movement began to teach that poverty does not equate to spirituality, many rejected this message as heresy. Even though there were some extreme teachings in the faith movement, many of the core revelations are now accepted throughout the body of Christ. For instance, many people who would never identify with the faith movement accept that there is great power and wisdom in praying and declaring God's Word over our lives and circumstances.

If there is one point I hope you receive deep into your spirit, it is this: *the battle for transformation takes place in our minds.* Romans 12:2 says, "And do not be conformed to this world, but be transformed by the renewing of your mind, that you may prove what is that good and acceptable and perfect will of God."

Now is the time for your life to be transformed by the revelation knowledge of God's grace. Now is the time to stop accepting something less than God's absolute best. Now is the time to press past the point of blessing to the place of breakthrough.

> The battle for transformation
> takes place in our minds.

As we proceed into this revelation, I urge you to clear your mind of every preconceived idea you may have about grace. Rid yourself of any limiting notions about

7

God's ability to bring you to a place of victory. Open your spirit to see God's grace and its power the way He always intended for you to understand it.

Remember the instruction we are given in 2 Corinthians 10:4, "Casting down imaginations, and every high thing that exalteth itself against the knowledge of God, and bringing into captivity every thought to the obedience of Christ" (KJV). Don't let any high thing stand between you and the revelation of the power God has given you through His grace. No more defeat, no more struggling, no more lack in any area. Now is your time! God is going to open the windows of heaven and reveal to you a place called grace, where everything you need is.

Chapter 2

BREAKING THROUGH
TO GOOD GROUND

I N ONE OF the greatest parables in Scripture, Jesus revealed to us the secret of the battle for truth and how to penetrate to the place of real breakthrough. In Luke 8 Jesus shares the parable of the sower:

> "A sower went out to sow his seed. And as he sowed, some fell by the wayside; and it was trampled down, and the birds of the air devoured it. Some fell on rock; and as soon as it sprang up, it withered away because it lacked moisture. And some fell among thorns, and the thorns sprang up with it and choked it. But others fell on good ground, sprang up, and yielded a crop a hundredfold." When He had said these things He cried, "He who has ears to hear, let him hear!"
>
> —LUKE 8:5–8

The word translated "hear" in this passage means to hear and understand. Jesus desperately wanted His disciples to understand the powerful truth in these verses, yet even to this day this truth has eluded many Christians.

I think it is telling—and a sign of wisdom—that the disciples sought Jesus for understanding even before He explained the parable. The Scriptures say, "Then His disciples asked Him, saying, 'What does this parable mean?' And He said, 'To you it has been given to know the mysteries of the kingdom of God'" (Luke 8:9–10). I pray that, like the disciples, you will eagerly seek after truth and open your spirit to receive a revelation.

> When He had said these things He cried, "He who has ears to hear, let him hear!" —Luke 8:8

Throughout most of my Christian experience I have heard it taught that Jesus was talking about four kinds of hearts in the parable of the sower: the wayside heart, the stony heart, the thorny heart, and the way our hearts should be, the good soil. Although there is a great truth in this teaching about the four types of hearts identified in this passage, I believe an even more significant truth is revealed in this parable.

I believe Jesus was not only exposing four different kinds of hearts, but He was also revealing four stages at which truth enters a person's heart. Each time we receive truth, it has to pass through these four stages in order to become full grown and mature. Let's take a look at each of these stages.

Stage One—the Stolen Seed

Stage one is the first time a new truth comes to us. Jesus explained what happens in this stage.

> The seed is the word of God. Those by the wayside are the ones who hear; then the devil comes and *takes away the word out of their hearts,* lest they should *believe and be saved.*
>
> —LUKE 8:11–12,
> emphasis added

First, to remove any possible confusion, the word *saved* in these verses, which is the Greek word *sozo,* means to be delivered or to be made whole in spirit, soul, and body. It is not simply talking about the word that leads to a born-again experience. Jesus is talking about the word that brings deliverance. Jesus prayed in John 17:17, "Sanctify them by Your truth. Your word is truth."

In the first stage the heart (the center of our thoughts and feelings) is not ready to receive truth. The Word of God came to those on the wayside, but their hearts were in such a condition that the devil was able to steal it before it could take root. This is significant. *The truth was stolen from their hearts and minds.*

How many times have we experienced this? The first time a new truth came to us we couldn't retain it. Before we walked out the door of the church, the devil through doubt, unbelief, fear, pride, or any of the other weapons in his arsenal stole the Word from us.

I remember the first time I heard the truth about tithing. I was only a few weeks old in the Lord. The moment I heard it, I rejected it. The Bible says, "He who

---

has ears to hear, let him hear" (Matt. 11:15; Mark 4:9; Rev. 2:29). I didn't have ears to hear. I couldn't understand why God wanted 10 percent of *my* income. I was a poor student. Surely God didn't want *me* to give 10 percent of *my* money to the church. Just as soon as the word came from the preacher's mouth, doubt and fear were robbing it from my heart and mind. That truth was falling by the wayside.

> The truth was stolen from their hearts and minds.

But truth is powerful. It did eventually take root and began a process of growth and maturity in me.

This has happened to me many times in my Christian walk. In the first church I attended as a new believer, the leaders preached against the faith movement. So the first time I heard Kenneth Copeland preach, I rejected everything he had to say. The truths he had to share were falling by the wayside. The devil, through unbelief and a critical spirit, was robbing me of some very powerful truths.

Regarding the tithing issue, because I lacked revelation of God's divine provision, I allowed fear to rob me of the power and blessings of tithing, which I now enjoy. I resisted the faith movement because the enemy used pride, expressed through a critical spirit that I received *in the church*, to keep me in bondage. To put Luke 8:11–12 in my own words, "Then the devil came and took *away the word out of Steve Foss's heart*, lest he should *believe and be saved* [be delivered and made whole]."

In this parable of the sower Jesus was exposing us to the first battlefront that the Word faces when it comes: a heart that is not open to receive. Many things cause our hearts to be closed to God's Word. I want to go through some of the more common ones.

Our traditions

Mark 7:13 says, "Making the *word of God of no effect through your tradition* which you have handed down. And many such things you do" (emphasis added). It is possible for us to put our traditions above the Word of God.

For example, Mark 16:17 says, "And these signs will follow those who believe: In My name they will cast out demons; they will speak with new tongues." But some church traditions claim tongues was only for the early church. Even though this word is for all believers, many can't receive it because their traditions have told them it isn't for today.

The same is true of healing. I was in a church once in the southern part of England. After I preached, I began to move around the room, praying for people to receive a fresh touch from God. I came upon a woman in a wheelchair. She hadn't walked in more than five years. Immediately I felt the Lord lead me to tell the woman to stand up because God was healing her. I said, "Stand up." She said, "I can't." I told her that the Lord was healing her and to stand up. Finally she slowly rose up out of that wheelchair. She took one step, then another, then suddenly she was running around the church building completely healed.

Her husband came up to me after the service. He told me his wife hadn't walked in five years, and even though she was running around the church, he said to me, "I don't believe she is healed." I guess he thought her ability to walk was only temporary. He proceeded to order his wife to sit back down in the wheelchair before she hurt herself. In the face of God's Word being demonstrated in his wife's life, this man's tradition, which told him God doesn't heal today, was robbing the word right out of his heart. For the next six months he ordered his wife to get back in that wheelchair, and she refused. Finally, she gave in to him and sat back in the wheelchair. Immediately she couldn't walk anymore. The devil through this husband's persecution had stolen the word of healing from the woman's heart.

Rebellion

Ezekiel 12:2 says, "Son of man, you dwell in the midst of a rebellious house, which has eyes to see but does not see, and ears to hear but does not hear; for they are a rebellious house." When we are in rebellion to God, we are spiritually blinded. As long as we are rejecting God's authority over areas of our lives, we are unable to see clearly the truths of God. This is one of the reasons this false grace message is sweeping the body of Christ today. There is a rebellion in the hearts of God's people toward His commands to live holy and separate from the world.

Many want to go to heaven but don't want to give up their sin. So when the Word is preached about living a holy, separated, and consecrated life, they can't receive it. They see it as bondage, not as the fruit of a Spirit-led and Spirit-controlled life. So they are unable to receive anything that seems to restrict them from the lifestyle they want to live. Then they begin to label certain portions of

God's Word and those who preach those truths as "religious" and "legalistic." The rebellion in their hearts has blinded them to the truth of God's Word. But "as He who called you is holy, you also be holy in all your conduct, because it is written, 'Be holy, for I am holy'" (1 Pet. 1:15–16).

Doctrines of men

Jesus said in Matthew 15:8–10, 12–14: "'These people draw near to Me with their mouth, and honor Me with their lips, but their heart is far from Me. And in vain they worship Me, *teaching as doctrines the commandments of men.*' When He had called the multitude to Himself, He said to them, 'Hear *and understand*'... Then His disciples came and said to Him, 'Do You know that the Pharisees were offended when they heard this saying?'...But He answered and said, 'Every plant which My heavenly Father has not planted will be uprooted. Let them alone. *They are blind leaders of the blind. And if the blind leads the blind, both will fall into a ditch*'" (emphasis added).

In contrast to the false grace message that seems to give people a license to sin, the doctrines of men fall on the other end of the spectrum. It is when church leaders add commandments and requirements to Scripture and make believers think they must follow those rules to truly be right with God. For instance, they tell people they must observe certain feasts or follow certain codes of conduct in order to garner the favor of God and be used by Him. I remember reading a book early in my Christian walk that said if a minister doesn't pray X number of hours each day, he wasn't worth his weight in salt. I knew I was called by God into the ministry, so I started to make sure I prayed at least that certain number of hours each day.

I was so bound by this doctrine that I would actually get up in the middle of the night to pray my extra fifteen minutes or so if I realized I hadn't met the full time requirement. I didn't believe I could be used of God if I missed any of my prayer time. I finally broke free from this doctrine of men when I was a counselor at a youth camp and literally had no time to pray because of my responsibilities. Although I wasn't able to pray that specific number of hours, I saw God use me to minister powerfully at that camp. That is when I realized that it wasn't spending X number of hours each day in prayer that was important; it was developing a lifestyle of prayer that really mattered.

Doubt

James 1:5–7 tells us, "If any of you lacks wisdom, let him ask of God, who gives to all liberally and without reproach, and it will be given to him. But let him ask in faith, with no doubting, for he who doubts is like a wave of the sea driven and tossed by the wind. *For let not that man suppose that he will receive anything from the Lord*" (emphasis added).

What will the man who doubts not receive? He will not receive revelation. Does this man not receive revelation because God is mean? No, he doesn't receive anything because doubt gives the devil power to steal the Word out of his heart. To doubt means to consider another thought. It is giving credence to something other than God's Word.

In receiving this revelation on grace, you are going to have to clear your mind of thoughts that would harden your heart against the truth of God's Word. The key to getting truth past this first stage and having a heart that is open to receive is humility. We must humble ourselves before God and His Word. In humility we must exalt God's Word above all our own thoughts and opinions. This simple act is what opens the door to revelation and breakthrough.

We see this modeled in Simon Peter's encounter with Jesus in Luke 5:

> When He had stopped speaking, He said to Simon, "Launch out into the deep and let down your nets for a catch." But Simon answered and said to Him, "*Master, we have toiled all night and caught nothing*; nevertheless *at Your word* I will let down the net." And when they had done this, they caught a great number of fish, and their net was breaking.
>
> —LUKE 5:4–6,
> emphasis added

Had Peter not humbled himself by exalting Jesus's word above his own thoughts and feelings, the devil would have stolen the word from his heart before it could produce anything. This is what happens to all of us when we are confronted with the Word. We will talk much more about humility later in this book. For now it is important that you understand that we always have a choice: we can either humble ourselves and receive the Word or hold on to our preconceived ways of thinking and allow the devil to steal it.

Stage Two—the Test of Failures

When Jesus was explaining the parable of the sower, Jesus told His disciples, "They on the rock are they, which, when they hear, receive the word with joy; and these have no root, which for a while believe, and in time of temptation fall away" (Luke 8:13, KJV). The word *temptation* in this verse means a trial, test, or adversity.

At this point in the journey to see truth break through, we have humbled ourselves and received the Word, and this has produced a feeling of joy in our lives. You can probably relate to the joy that comes with discovering and receiving truth.

When I left the service where I first heard about tithing, the devil had already tried to rob me of the truth I had just heard. I asked a new church friend of mine about the principles of tithing we had just been taught. Although I was full of doubt and fear, I had already seen God do so many wondrous things in my life that I knew if tithing was in His Word, I wanted to obey. As my friend taught me the principles of tithing, my fear and doubt turned to pure joy and excitement as I received and yielded to the truth. I couldn't wait to go to the next church service so I could give my first tithe.

In this second stage of receiving truth, you have received the Word, but you haven't yet become experienced in the usage of the Word. You have joy over the Word, but you haven't learned how to walk in the power of that Word continually. Often when people first start tithing, they don't see overnight prosperity. They may see some initial fruit, but then many times their finances will get attacked. They will get hit with financial difficulty that will make them question the validity of God's Word.

Often when this happens they will back away from the truth and fail to press on until they get past the trial. They believe God for a while, but when adversity comes, they fall away from that particular truth.

Many people fall away from certain truths without turning away from their saving knowledge of Christ. They still trust God for their salvation, but they no longer trust Him for financial provision, healing, deliverance, household salvation, and so on. Peter faced this same battle.

> Now in the fourth watch of the night Jesus went to them, walking on the sea. And when the disciples saw Him walking on the sea, they were troubled, saying, "It is a ghost!" And they cried out for fear. But immediately Jesus spoke to them, saying, "Be of good cheer! It is I; do not be afraid." And Peter answered Him and said, *"Lord, if it is You, command me to come to You on the water."* So *He said, "Come."* And when Peter had come down out of the boat, *he walked on the water to go to Jesus.* But *when he saw that the wind was boisterous*, he was afraid; and *beginning to sink he cried out, saying, "Lord, save me!"* And immediately Jesus stretched out His hand and caught him, and said to him, *"O you of little faith, why did you doubt?"*
> —MATTHEW 14:25–31,
> emphasis added

Peter had received the Word. Jesus said, "Come," and he stepped out of the boat and walked on the water.

19

What joy and excitement must have been surging through him! Can you imagine his emotions? Then he noticed the winds and the waves. Although he was now walking on the water and experiencing the power of the Word, he didn't know how to continue walking in faith when confronted with adversity.

Peter began to sink. Now can you imagine what he must have felt? Fear, terror, and unbelief. However, though he took his eyes off Jesus and began focusing on the problem, Peter did do something right in this situation. While facing this stage of trial that knocks out so many, Peter could have cried out to his friends in the boat. He could have begun to try to swim frantically. But he responded correctly to his mistake. Peter did the only wise thing he could do when he found himself beginning to sink; he cried out to Jesus.

We all have experienced what Peter endured. We have had the joy and excitement of receiving truth for the first time. And we have all felt the fear and unbelief that comes when that Word is challenged with adversity. The key to passing through this stage is to do what Peter did. We must cry out to Jesus. We all fail at times, but Jesus is there to pick us up. Now, when He does, He is likely to rebuke us. Jesus will expose why we failed, but He does this so we can grow and avoid making the same mistake again.

If we humble ourselves and receive His correction, we will be saved (delivered) from the root issues in our hearts that caused us to fail. God will not only rescue us from the failure as He did Peter when He pulled him out of the water, but He will also rescue us from the root that caused the failure, which in Peter's case was doubt.

Jesus reached for Peter, lifted him out of the water, and said, "O you of little faith, why did you doubt?" (v. 31). This could also be read, "O you of short-lasting faith, why did you think another thought or consider another word besides Mine."

The word *little* here means short in duration, not small in amount. Jesus was saying to Peter, "Why did you have short-lasting faith? I told you to come. I gave you My Word. Why did you consider another thought?"

The same thing could have been said to me and probably to you too at some point in our lives. On so many occasions we received a revelation of truth. We started to see it bear fruit in our lives, but when push came to shove we considered another thought. We looked at our circumstances instead of to Jesus, and we began to sink.

Every truth you receive will face this test of failures, the test where it seems that the word won't keep you, protect you, sustain you, or provide for you. In order for you to move into the place where the word produces what God intended it to in your life, the revelation truth will have to pass through stage two: the test of failures.

Stage Three—the Test of Success

Luke 8:14 describes the third stage truth must pass through: "Now the ones that fell among thorns are those who, when they have heard, go out and are choked with *cares, riches, and pleasures of life*, and bring *no fruit to maturity*" (emphasis added). This third stage is a unique one at which many people mistakenly think they have it all figured out.

They seem to have the favor of God all over their lives. It seems that everything they touch turns to gold. If they

21

are in ministry, people from all over the world may be coming to learn from them. Their financial needs are met. They receive honor from men, fame, recognition, power, and influence. They begin to feel as if they have it all, and in a way they do. They have learned how to apply the Word. They have learned how to persevere in the face of adversity and trust in Jesus. The Word begins to prosper abundantly in their lives. They have a joy that brings with it confidence and steadfastness. These individuals are not easily shaken. They have prayed, fasted, sought God, and now they see the fruit—and the fruit is *big.* They are reaping a great harvest, or so they think.

What most people at this stage don't realize is that the place where their faithfulness begins to bear fruit isn't the end of the journey. It's just another testing ground. As biblical and church history has taught us, success often brings along some nasty friends. In Luke 8:14 we see that "the ones that fell among thorns are those who, when they have heard, go out and are choked with *cares, riches,* and *pleasures of life,* and bring *no fruit to maturity*" (emphasis added).

There are three areas Jesus warns His disciples to watch out for during the test of success. The first area is *cares.* This word does not mean "worries," as many today would misinterpret. The word *cares* in this verse means distractions. It is so easy when things are going well to become distracted. We finally get some success, so we begin to cruise a little. We feel we can take a little break. We think we don't have to sacrifice as much.

When success comes, we often let down our guard. That is why it's so easy to become distracted from the pure and holy call of God when money, fame, and favor have come our way. This has happened throughout history. Look at the Israelites. They would experience the favor and abundance of God only to quickly forget who brought them the favor and abundance, because they allowed themselves to be distracted by things such as what the nations around them were doing, their customs and idols.

The second area is the *deceitfulness of riches*. Beloved, don't be fooled. Although money isn't evil, money has destroyed many good men and women. There is a deceitfulness that comes with wealth. Financial abundance has a way of causing us to stop depending on God. When wealth comes, we have a tendency to lean on its power to get what we want.

Oh, we Christians may pursue wealth in the name of God. We may say we want resources to build a worship center or to help those in need, but often deep down we want wealth to satisfy our own selfish purposes. While there is nothing wrong with money and wealth, we must guard against trusting in riches to supply our needs instead of God.

The third area, which ties the other two together, is the *pleasures of this life*. We see this all around us in the church from the pulpit to the pew. Several years ago my family and I were out house hunting. We drove into a very nice community with huge homes. There were several open houses in the neighborhood. The homes were stunning on the outside. As we walked in, the foyers were huge with twenty-five-foot ceilings, massive chandeliers, and ornate décor.

As we walked through these five-thousand- to six-thousand-square-foot homes that we later found out were listed for around a million dollars, I had a very sick feeling in my spirit. I told my wife that I didn't like these homes at all. I have been around wealth and have stayed in some of the finest hotels in the world when speaking at conferences. I am not bothered by wealth, but this troubled me. When I asked my wife, Carrie, about why I was feeling so uneasy, she spoke with words of divine revelation.

She said that these homes were not for "living" in; they were for the flaunting of wealth. I said, "That's it! That's what's bothering me!"

The Bible clearly teaches us to do all things in moderation. Excess is the playground of the devil. When we, during times of "blessing," give ourselves over to the lust of this life, we fall into a trap of the enemy that will choke out the revelation Word of God.

When blessings become curses

I was up early one morning praying when the Lord spoke something very powerful to me. He said: "Tell My people I am about to pour out My abundance like never before. Many will rejoice because they think it is My favor, but warn them because it will be their greatest test. Son, many who stand during the test of failures will fall under the test of success, for success will expose things in their hearts that were never exposed during their times of failure."

This is also what happened to Peter. By the time Peter had been with Jesus for several years, he had grown very strong. Jesus had declared him to be the rock and the leader of the church. Clearly he had favor with Christ. He was able to go places with Jesus that most didn't.

He was on the Mount of Transfiguration where he saw Moses and Elijah. He was enveloped in the glory of God and heard the audible voice of the Lord. Peter cast out devils, healed the sick, performed miracles; his ministry was taking off.

In the midst of this success he felt he had the power to overcome anything. We read in Luke 22:33, "But he said to Him, *'Lord, I am ready to go with You, both to prison and to death'*" (emphasis added). Peter believed he had enough spiritual power and experience to face anything. However, Jesus knew the depths of his heart: "Then He said, 'I tell you, Peter, the rooster shall not crow this day before you will deny three times that you know Me'" (v. 34).

Peter did have favor and power in God. He was prospering and beginning to walk in his calling. Yet he had one thing that he didn't realize: he still loved his life more than Christ. He thought success was the sign that he had arrived. He was wrong. The "success" was simply bringing him to the greatest test of his life. In the midst of success and power could you die to yourself, your dreams, your life?

The answer for Peter was no. He failed and ended up running and hiding. Thanks be to God for His mercies, though. Jesus, after the resurrection, once again exposed Peter's sin and the root of his failures. Jesus said, "Simon, son of Jonas, lovest thou me more than these?" (John 21:15, KJV).

> In the midst of success and power, could you die to yourself, your dreams, your life?

Peter replied, "Yea, Lord; thou knowest that I love thee" (v. 15, KJV). But Peter didn't yet understand what Jesus was asking him. Peter needed to know that if he was ever to go to the place where his seed produced thirty, sixty, and a hundredfold, he was going to have to die to self.

In John 12:24–25 Jesus tells His disciples, "Most assuredly, I say to you, unless a grain of wheat falls into the ground and dies, it remains alone; but if it dies, it produces much grain. He who loves his life will lose it, and he who hates his life in this world will keep it for eternal life."

This is the key to passing the test of success. Even when God's favor and blessing are abundant, we can never love this world. We will never produce as much for God's kingdom if we are not willing to lose our lives and give up everything for Him.

Stage Four—Dead Men Walking

This final stage is where the Word of God—the revelation of truth—will truly begin to produce what God always intended. This is the place where Christ will increase and our flesh will decrease. This is the place where we will no longer desire fame, fortune, the praise of men, or titles and positions. When God's people have arrived at the place where they are dead men walking, they won't be acting as celebrity Christians who flaunt their ministries as if they are God's gift to men.

This is the place where we have died to self and are living only for Him. Only when we come to this place will we see God produce fruit in our lives at the thirty, sixty, and a hundredfold. This is the place where people will see Jesus in us and be drawn to Him.

I wanted to spend some time laying this foundation before I began talking about grace for a very important reason. The amazing truths about grace in this book will have to pass through these four stages in order for them to truly bring forth mature fruit in your life. You're going to have to be willing to allow the Word to challenge your preconceived thoughts, doctrines, and feelings about grace. You're going to have to humble yourself before God and say, "Lord, teach me."

If you want a quick fix for all of your spiritual woes, as if such a thing exists, you have the wrong book. If all you want is a microwave spiritual maturity, do yourself a favor and put this book down and never come back to it. To him who has been given much, much is required. Once you receive the revelation in this book, you will be held responsible for how you respond to the truth you have been given.

But if you are ready to enter into the journey of a lifetime down the path of divine revelation, then let's get started, for there is a place called grace where everything you need is.

Chapter 3

WHAT GRACE REALLY IS

THE APOSTLE PETER writes:

> Grace and peace be multiplied unto you through the knowledge of God, and of Jesus our Lord, according as his divine power hath given unto us all things that pertain unto life and godliness, through the knowledge of him that hath called us to glory and virtue.
>
> —2 PETER 1:2–3, KJV

Grace is not simply some kind of ethereal blessing by which we are saved. As you will discover through this book, it is a place—a place where we will no longer struggle. It's a place where we will have total provision and continual supply. In this chapter we are going to venture a little further down the road to discovering this place called grace.

In order to understand true grace, we are going to have to allow the Word to challenge our understanding and remove any inaccurate beliefs. In the last chapter we talked about the roadblocks to receiving truth. I wanted to lay that foundation before we began this journey, because in order to receive this message we must be willing to pass through the stages of revelation—from the wayside to stony ground, through thorny places, and ultimately to good, tilled soil. Only then will we see the fruit that God has promised. There are no quick fixes; we grow in the knowledge of His grace line upon line and precept upon precept.

Although many people find grace complicated, in reality, it is simple to understand. Notice that 2 Peter 1:3 says Christ's *"divine power hath given unto us all things that pertain unto life and godliness"* (KJV, emphasis added). Simply put, grace is the favor of God that gives us access to the power of God for everything we need for life and godliness.

I want you to consider that statement again: *Grace is the favor of God that gives us access to the power of God for everything we need for life and godliness.* That is not a complicated idea. The reason many Christians often find it difficult to understand grace is that they confuse it with mercy.

Grace is the undeserved, unearned favor of God that gives us access to the power of God for everything we need for life and godliness. Mercy is when we have sinned and deserve judgment, yet because of the blood of Jesus we don't receive the punishment we should receive.

Grace gives us favor to access the power of God; mercy releases us from the judgment of God. Grace is favor. That favor gives us access. Grace gives us the legal right to access the power of God for everything we need. Romans 3:23 says, "For all have sinned, and come short of the glory of God" (KJV). And in Romans 3:10 we read, "As it is written, There is none righteous, no, not one" (KJV). None of us deserve access to God and His power. Because of sin

29

we all deserve an everlasting hell. And yet God has given us access to all that He is and all that He has.

This truth became clear to me in December of 1999. My church, River of Life in Corona, California, was in the midst of a genuine outpouring of the Holy Spirit. We were seeking God as we never had before. I was praying on average more than five hours a day. We were holding services five nights a week. Never in my life had I sought God with such fervency. Never had I so separated myself from the things of the world. Never had I lived as holy a life as I did during this time.

> Grace is the favor of God that gives us access to the power of God for everything we need for life and godliness.

On December 30, 1999, we were near the end of a service. Once again the presence of God had been incredibly rich. I was sitting on the edge of the platform getting ready to dismiss the service when suddenly the presence of God came upon me powerfully. I fell straight back and was lying on the platform. I couldn't move. I was literally frozen in place for thirty minutes or so.

While I was on the ground, one of the men in our church came over and grabbed my feet and prayed for me. About ten minutes after he finished praying, I felt another person grab my feet. It was gentle at first and then quite firm. As this second set of hands held my feet, my body began to shake. When the hands lifted off of my feet, I could move my whole body again.

After further investigation I found out that nobody

had grabbed my feet the second time—at least nobody people could see. When I finally sat up, the Lord spoke something to me that would forever change my life. He said, "You have sought Me like never before. You have lived holier than at any other time in your life. You have pursued My presence far beyond any other time in your life. You think you are worthy to receive the outpouring of My glory. *However, during this time, your sin is worthy of eternal damnation.*"

In the natural I felt that no one could have pointed a finger at my life. I was doing everything I knew to do to be pleasing to God. I felt my motives were pure. All I truly wanted was Him. Yet even in this state I still had sin in my life. I still fell short of the glory and holiness of God, and the sin in my life, as all sin, was detestable to God. It was deserving of His judgment and warranted an eternity in hell.

Although I had preached that the sin we commit even as Christians is repugnant to God and worthy of hell, I never really saw it until that night. I had a true, deep revelation that even as a Christian I still fell far short of the glory and righteousness of God. I had believed this as part of the doctrine I had been taught, but now I had a real revelation of this truth. The words the Lord spoke that night shook me to the core of my being.

Yet while He was still speaking those words, I heard the Lord speaking in a second voice. The first voice spoke to me person to person. The second voice echoed through the heavens. In a second, simultaneous voice He said, "But *My mercy* endures forever."

At that moment I knew that if God's mercies were ever to cease, I would be a goner. I knew that without

His everlasting mercy, I couldn't survive one moment. His mercies cover me! Praise the name of the Lord!

Mercy is when we are released from the judgment we deserve. God has shown us mercy by not making us pay the penalty for our sin. Even though we sin, He releases us from the judgment it warrants when we repent and believe in Jesus. As long as we remain in Christ, that mercy keeps us from the judgment we truly deserve. We all need His mercy, and that mercy will endure forever. Yet we are not saved by mercy. We are saved by grace.

Grace is the favor of God that gives us access to the power of God for everything we need. Grace gave me the favor of God to get access to His mercies, without which I could never survive. Hebrews 4:16 says, "Let us therefore come boldly to the *throne of grace, that we may obtain mercy* and find grace to help in time of need" (emphasis added). Without the grace (the favor) of God, we could never have access to the mercy of God.

God favored us while we were yet sinners. This is very important for you to understand. *God first released His grace before He was able to extend to us His mercy.* Romans 5:8 tells us, "But God demonstrates His love toward us, in that *while we were still sinners, Christ died for us*" (emphasis added).

We didn't deserve the favor of God. We deserved hell. But God so loved us, He placed such value on us that, while we were His enemies, He sent Jesus to die for us that we might have *access* to Him. With that access to Him we now can receive mercy for all our sins. It is this access that comes to us undeserved and unearned, which has allowed us to be forgiven, cleansed, and made a new creation.

If God hadn't given us favor to access His power, we could never be free but would be bound for all eternity to death and destruction. Satan's goal in the Garden of Eden was to cause sin to enter the world so that mankind would no longer have access to the eternal power of God for everything we would need for life and godliness. He knew that if man sinned, we could no longer eat from the tree of life—the tree of total provision and continual supply.

The apostle Paul wrote:

> That at that time *you were without Christ*, being aliens from the commonwealth of Israel and strangers from the covenants of promise, *having no hope and without God in the world.* But now *in Christ Jesus you who once were far off have been brought near by the blood of Christ.* For He Himself is our peace, who has made both one, and has broken down the middle wall of separation, having abolished in His flesh the enmity, that is, the law of commandments contained in ordinances, so as to create in Himself one new man from the two, thus making peace, and that He might reconcile them both to God in one body through the cross, thereby putting to death the enmity. And He came and preached peace to you who were afar off and to those who were near. *For through Him we both have access* by one Spirit *to the Father.*
> —Ephesians 2:12–18,
> emphasis added

Through His Grace

The grace of God gives back to us access to God's power for everything we need. All the things we receive from God come to us *through His grace*.

We are saved through grace.

Acts 15:11 says, "But we believe that *through the grace* of the Lord Jesus Christ we shall be saved in the same manner as they" (emphasis added). We know that through the grace of the Lord Jesus Christ, we shall be saved.

We believe through grace.

We read in Acts 18:27, "And when he was minded to pass over into Achaia, the brethren encouraged him, and wrote to the disciples to receive him: and when he was come, he helped them much that had *believed through grace*" (ASV, emphasis added). We're saved by grace, and the Bible says we have the ability to believe by grace. How often do we struggle with unbelief? The Bible says that the power to believe comes by grace.

> All the things we receive from God come to us *through His grace*.

We receive our inheritance by grace.

Acts 20:32 says, "And now I commend you to God, and to the word of his grace, which is able to build you up, and to give you the inheritance among all them that are sanctified" (ASV). Although we deserve only an eternity in hell, Jesus not only saved us, but He also left us an inheritance. Through grace we're built up, we become strong, and we receive our inheritance.

Through grace and the access we have to God's power, we are built up; we are developed into the permanent dwelling place of God. Ephesians 2:22 says, "In whom you also are being built together for a dwelling place of God in the Spirit." You're being built up into your inheritance. Your inheritance is not comprised of things. It is "Christ in you, the hope of glory" (Col. 1:27). Your inheritance is that you have been predestined by God to be changed into His image.

Grace is the favor of God that gives us access to the power of God so we can be transformed into the image of Christ. Only as we receive God's favor can we access God's glory and behold Him. When we are able to come before Him, we are changed into His image. We read in 2 Corinthians 3:18, "And all of us, as with unveiled face, [because we] continued to behold [in the Word of God] as in a mirror the glory of the Lord, are constantly being transfigured into His very own image in ever increasing splendor and from one degree of glory to another; [for this comes] from the Lord [Who is] the Spirit" (AMP). Grace is the favor of God that gives us access to the power of God so we can claim our inheritance.

We obey by grace.

The Bible says through God's grace we receive the power to obey. Romans 1:5 says, "Through whom we *received grace and apostleship, unto obedience* of faith among all the nations, for his name's sake" (ASV, emphasis added). In so many churches Christians are beaten over the head with rules and regulations. They are told that they have to do this and do that in order to be pleasing to God, and then they feel defeated when they struggle to obey. The Bible tells us that God's grace gives us the power to obey; it is not something we do of ourselves. So many people are living in condemnation because they don't have a revelation that grace gives them access to the power of God so they can obey the will of God.

We stand by grace.

It is grace that gives us the power—the ability—to stand against the devil. Romans 5:2 tells us, "Through whom also we have had our access by faith into this grace *wherein we stand*; and we rejoice in hope of the glory of God" (ASV, emphasis added). A lot of people say they can't resist temptation. That's a lie from the pit of hell, because grace—God's grace—will give us the power to stand.

We receive spiritual gifts by grace.

All the gifts of the Spirit are received by grace. Romans 12:6 says, *"And having gifts differing according to the grace* that was given to us, whether prophecy, let us prophesy according to the proportion of our faith" (ASV, emphasis added).

People often look at me and think I am special. They think I have a special calling and special gifts, and that is why I see the power and anointing of God operating in my life. They don't realize that I was kicked out of high school six weeks before graduation or that I spent five years abusing drugs and alcohol, stealing money from employers, friends, and family to pay for my drug habit.

They don't know the sexual misconduct I was involved in. They have no idea how lost I was.

Now I travel all over the world ministering to millions of people. Lives are changed; people are saved, healed, and set free. In our meetings we have seen the kinds of manifestations of God that I used to only read about in books on revival. None of this happens because I am "*so spiritual.*" It happens because of God's grace.

God Has Given to Us All Things

Everything you need comes by grace, which is God's favor on your life, regardless of whether you deserve it or not. However, if this is true, why do most of us live lives that are broke, defeated, sick, and without power?

It is because we don't understand the grace of God. We have failed to understand what grace is and how it can be multiplied in our lives. Through grace, we have favor that gives us access to the power of God for *all* things.

> Everything you need comes by grace, which is God's favor on your life, regardless of whether you deserve it or not.

God so loved the world that He made a choice. He gave. He gave Jesus, and the Bible says that if God did not spare His own Son, would He not freely give to you and me all things (Rom. 8:32)?

Let's look again at 2 Peter 1:2–3 in the American Standard Version:

> Grace to you and peace be multiplied in the knowledge of God and of Jesus our Lord; seeing that his divine power hath granted unto us all things that pertain unto life and godliness.

All things that pertain unto life—that means everything we need for life has been given to us: clothes, money, relationships, food, spiritual food, strength to stand against the devil, an ability to obey God, the power to cast out demons and heal the sick. Don't tell me that you can't live a godly life, that you can't live for God, that you can't remain pure and save yourself for your husband or wife. Don't tell me that you can't avoid drugs, drinking, or listening to ungodly music.

You say, "Brother Steve, it's too hard." No, you don't understand. Everything we need for life and for godliness has been given to us through God's divine power. Everything you need to live the life God desires for you has been given to you already.

The key to obtaining the power of God is *access*. One day I was having lunch with a very famous international minister. This man is powerfully anointed, and everybody wants to get close to him. He is also a very private man.

After lunch he pulled me aside from the other ministers, many of whom were also well-known, and talked with me privately. He just wanted to give me private access. He told me that I could call him anytime, which is something he rarely ever does.

He was giving me access. I don't deserve it. I definitely wasn't the most well-known person at the table, but he chose to give to me undeserved access. He showed me favor.

God has given you and me access to His very presence and power. Through His undeserved grace/favor, God has chosen to give us the legal right to tap into His power for everything we need. After reading this book, if you live a defeated Christian life, you will live it only because you choose to—because you're going to receive enough knowledge in these pages to cause the level of grace you are currently living in to multiply.

Chapter 4

GRACE BEING MULTIPLIED

W E HAVE ALREADY seen that grace is the favor of God that gives us access to the power of God for everything we need for life and godliness. But there is another incredible truth revealed in 2 Peter 1.

> Grace and peace *be multiplied* to you in the knowledge of God and of Jesus our Lord, as His divine power has given to us all things that pertain to life and godliness, through the knowledge of Him who called us by glory and virtue.
>
> —2 PETER 1:2–3,
> emphasis added

Peter tells us in this passage that grace can increase in our lives. It can actually be multiplied as we grow in the knowledge of God. This truth shatters holes in the concept that grace is a sovereign act of God totally void of human involvement. Let me explain.

We know that man has the power to reject knowledge. Hosea 4:6 says, "My people are destroyed for lack of knowledge: because thou hast *rejected knowledge*, I will also reject thee" (KJV, emphasis added).

Mankind also has the power and responsibility to accept, grow in, and search out knowledge. We read in the Book of Proverbs:

> So that thou incline thine ear unto wisdom, and apply thine heart to understanding; yea, if thou criest after knowledge, and liftest up thy voice for understanding; if thou seekest her as silver, and searchest for her as for hid treasures; then shalt thou understand the fear of the LORD, and find the knowledge of God. For the LORD giveth wisdom: out of his mouth cometh knowledge and understanding.
>
> —PROVERBS 2:2–6, KJV

The more revelation we walk in, the more grace we have to access the power of God.

The knowledge that we must seek out is not just information or scriptural indoctrination. The knowledge we must seek is revelation. Peter is saying that grace is multiplied in our lives through the revelation knowledge of God and our Lord Jesus Christ.

The more revelation we walk in, the more grace we have to access the power of God. I deal with the subject of growing in wisdom and revelation in great detail in my book *Satan's Dirty Little Secret*, but it needs to at least be touched on here.

The Spirit of Revelation

In Ephesians 1:17 Paul writes, "That the God of our Lord Jesus Christ, the Father of glory, may give unto you the spirit of wisdom and revelation in the knowledge of him" (KJV). The Amplified Bible puts it this way: "[For I always pray to] the God of our Lord Jesus Christ, the Father of glory, that He may grant you a spirit of wisdom and revelation *[of insight into mysteries and secrets] in the [deep and intimate] knowledge of Him*" (emphasis added).

This was not just the prayer of the apostle Paul; it was the prayer of the Holy Spirit. Second Timothy 3:16 tells us that "all Scripture is given by inspiration of God." And we read in 2 Peter 1:20–21, "Knowing this first, that no prophecy of Scripture is of any private interpretation, for prophecy never came by the will of man, but holy men of God spoke *as they were moved by the Holy Spirit*" (emphasis added).

This prayer in Ephesians 1 was from God and was intended for the most spiritual people of Paul's day. It was not for the baby Christians. The Ephesian church was the most mature group in Paul's day, and the Book of Ephesians has some of the most profound teaching on the purpose for the existence of the church in the Scriptures.

It is to these people that Paul writes: "[For I always pray to] the God of our Lord Jesus Christ, the Father of glory, that *He may grant you a spirit of wisdom and revelation* [of insight into mysteries and secrets] in the [deep and intimate] knowledge of Him" (Eph. 1:17, AMP, emphasis added).

In this verse Paul prays the prayer of the Holy Spirit that God the Father would give the Ephesian church a spirit of wisdom and revelation. Now there is only one Holy Spirit, so what Paul is talking about here is an anointing—a supernatural power for wisdom and revelation "[of insight into mysteries and secrets] in the [deep and intimate] knowledge of Him."

Paul in essence is saying, "You need something more than what you have, and everything you get comes by grace. The way to have grace multiplied in your life is through revelation knowledge. I am asking the Father to give you a supernatural ability to gain the knowledge of God so you can have more access to the power of God for everything you need for life and godliness."

God has secrets, and He wants to reveal them to us. Consider the following verses:

> He who dwells in the *secret place of the Most High* shall abide under the shadow of the Almighty.
> —PSALM 91:1,
> emphasis added

> But *there is a God in heaven who reveals secrets*, and He has made known to King Nebuchadnezzar what will be in the latter days. Your dream, and the visions of your head upon your bed, were these.
> —DANIEL 2:28,
> emphasis added

> *Then I will give them heart to know Me*, that I am the LORD; and they shall be My people, and I will be their God, for they shall return to Me with their whole heart.
> —JEREMIAH 24:7,
> emphasis added

> But as it is written: *"Eye has not seen, nor ear heard, nor have entered into the heart of man the things which God has prepared for those who love Him."*

> *But God has revealed them to us through His Spirit.*
> For the Spirit searches all things, yes, the deep
> things of God.
>
> —1 Corinthians 2:9–10,
> emphasis added

We need supernatural eyesight to see and understand the mysteries and secrets of God. But God *wants* us to know His secrets. God said in Jeremiah 29:13, "And you will seek Me and find Me, when you search for Me with all your heart."

Why does God want us to know His secrets? We find the answer in Deuteronomy 29:29: "The secret things belong to the Lord our God, but *those things which are revealed belong to us* and to our children forever" (emphasis added).

The secrets of the Lord belong to Him until they are revealed. Before I got saved, salvation was a mystery to me. I didn't know that I needed to be born again. But on May 2, 1986, the mystery of salvation was revealed to me, and I discovered that if I simply yielded to the truth I had learned, I would be saved.

Every year I used to catch a cold. I expected to get sick like clockwork. I was a Bible-believing Christian. I understood salvation, but I hadn't yet discovered the mystery of Isaiah 53:5: "But He was wounded for our transgressions, He was bruised for our iniquities; the chastisement for our peace was upon Him, *and by His stripes we are healed*" (emphasis added).

Grace (favor that gives us access to God's power) is multiplied through the revelation knowledge of God. As long as Isaiah 53:5 was a mystery, as long as I didn't have the fullness of this revelation, I could not tap into the favor that gives us access to the power of God for healing.

Once the mystery of the healing power of Christ's stripes was revealed, I began to access His healing power. I began to declare, "I am healed!" I stopped expecting to get sick, and I haven't gotten a cold since. It's been twelve years now.

When you see it—when the mystery is revealed—you can have it. Once the mystery is revealed, you can take possession of what is rightfully yours. It is your inheritance. An inheritance that is not understood does the heir no good. It is not until the heir sees and understands what is rightfully his that he can obtain it.

Paul by the Holy Spirit in Ephesians is praying that God will give you supernatural eyesight into mysteries and secrets in the deep and intimate knowledge of God. Once you see the secrets, you have legal access to them, for upon salvation we become "joint heirs with Christ" (Rom. 8:17). The only thing keeping us from possessing that inheritance is a lack of revelation knowledge.

One of the jobs of the Holy Spirit is to show us the secrets of God. Jesus told His disciples in John 16:

> However, when He, the Spirit of truth, has come, *He will guide you into all truth*; for He will not speak on His own authority, but whatever He hears He will speak; and He will tell you things to come. He will glorify Me, for *He will take of what is Mine and declare it to you*.
>
> —JOHN 16:13–14,
> emphasis added

45

God wants to open your spiritual eyes—the eyes of your heart, the eyes of your understanding—so you can really *see*. Ephesians 1:18 says, "Having the eyes of your heart flooded with light, so that you can know and understand the hope to which He has called you" (AMP). God has given us two sets of eyes. We have our natural eyes, but we also have spiritual eyes. We will see things with our spiritual eyes that our natural eyes will never see.

It is significant that the prayer of the Holy Spirit in Ephesians 1:18 is that "the eyes of your heart" be "flooded with light." We read in 2 Corinthians 4:6, "For it is the God who commanded light to shine out of darkness, who has shone in our hearts to give the *light of the knowledge of the glory of God* in the face of Jesus Christ" (emphasis added). Through the revealing of the knowledge of God, we gain greater access to the power of God.

> Grace and peace be multiplied to you in the knowledge of God and of Jesus our Lord. —2 Peter 1:2

I pray that God will grant to you the spirit of wisdom and revelation, that He would anoint the eyes of your understanding to see the mysteries and secrets of God. This is probably one of the biggest voids in the body of Christ today. We need to the light of revelation. Simply put, *we need to see Jesus.*

Chapter 5

REVELATION GIFTS

L ET'S TAKE ANOTHER look at our key passage in 2 Peter:

> *Grace* and peace *be multiplied to you in the knowledge of God and of Jesus our Lord,* as His divine power has given to us all things that pertain to life and godliness, *through the knowledge of Him* who called us by glory and virtue.
>
> —2 PETER 1:2–3,
> emphasis added

If grace increases based on our revelation knowledge of God, as these verses say, then you and I are directly involved in the amount of grace at work in our lives. We are active participants in this knowledge-multiplying process. If we do not search, seek, and accept the knowledge of God, then we will not see the increase of God's grace, which provides us with all things. Matthew 7:7 tells us, "Seek, and you will find."

In this chapter we are going to venture into some territory that makes some people uncomfortable. Those who have an independent spirit probably aren't going to like what I have to say in this chapter. Although I strongly believe that a person can and will receive much revelation through his personal prayer and study times with the Lord, those who do not understand and properly relate to this next truth usually do not receive as much revelation as God would have for them. Sometimes they fall into extremes. And, sadly, though these people often think they have "deep" insights into God, the reality is that they have no real power at work in their lives, and the world around them is not changed. If we don't enter into and come under the influence of this next truth, we will never grow into maturity.

Grace According to the Gift

Ephesians 4:7 tells us, "But to each one of us grace was given according to the measure of Christ's gift." We have already seen that grace is multiplied in our lives through the revelation knowledge of God. Now we see Paul saying here that grace comes in measures, and it is according to something.

According is the pivotal word here. It is pointing us to a revelation that is about to be made clear in the next few verses. *Kata* is the Greek preposition that is translated "according to" in this verse. The word is meant to connect two things; in this case it is connecting grace with the gift of Christ.

The measure of the gift of Christ determines the amount of grace given to us individually. So then where and what is the gift of Christ?

Ephesians 4:8 says, "Therefore He says: 'When He ascended on high, He led captivity captive, and *gave gifts to men*'" (emphasis added). Grace comes in measures according to the *gifts* that are in men (and women). Grace is given to us according to the gift of Christ, and Jesus gave those gifts to men.

Everything we need that pertains to life and godliness comes from grace, and grace is multiplied through revelation knowledge, which comes from the gifts that God has placed inside of men. So who are these men and women through whom grace is given? Let's look a little further down in Ephesians.

> And he gave some, *apostles*; and some, *prophets*; and some, *evangelists*; and some, *pastors and teachers*; for the *perfecting* of the saints, for the work of the ministry, for the edifying of the body of Christ.
>
> —EPHESIANS 4:11-12, KJV,
> emphasis added

Grace is given to us according to the gift of Christ, and Jesus gave those gifts to men.

Why did He give some apostles, some prophets, some evangelists, and some pastors and teachers? For the "perfecting," or as some translations say, for the "equipping," of the saints for the work of the ministry.

Grace is the favor of God that gives us *access*. How can we be perfected and equipped if we don't have access? And how can we have access if we lack revelation knowledge?

God has put gifts inside of apostles, prophets, evangelists, pastors, and teachers to reveal to you the knowledge of God, because He knows that this knowledge will bring you to a place called grace, where you'll have everything you need. You'll be perfected and equipped. For what? So that you might do the work of the ministry—so you can go into the world, make disciples, and do everything God has called you to do. This is not the only way revelation comes. As I said before, we can receive much revelation through our personal prayer and Bible study times. But if we don't know how to receive from the men and women of God who are put in our lives, we will not access the fullness of revelation God intended for us to have.

Receiving the Ministry Gifts

You won't be properly equipped to make disciples until you receive from the gift of God. You can't fully accomplish all God has for you until you accept and appreciate the gifts He has given men and allow them to help you grow. Jeremiah 3:15 says, "And I will give you shepherds according to My heart, who will feed you with knowledge and understanding."

As we see in Scripture, God has established a structure through which all His blessings will flow. God has made us mutually dependent on one another. Many people think all that matters is their individual relationship with God, that He will reveal to them the truth so long as they pray and seek Him. But God has a set authority structure through which He will flow.

When I'm on the platform preaching, I stand there as a vessel. As I begin to preach that Jesus came to save, heal, and deliver, grace is released to those who are open to receive from the ministry gift that is flowing through me. As you receive what I am teaching in this book, grace (favor for access to power) is being released to you so that you can enter into the experience of what is being taught. It is as we submit to the authority and receive from the gift inside the apostle, prophet, evangelist, pastor, or teacher that grace is multiplied unto us.

The gift of Christ inside the fivefold minister is there to bring a dimension of the revelation of Christ to the saints. Inside the true fivefold minister is a gift given from Christ Jesus to release favor onto the saints so they can access the power of God for everything they need for life and godliness.

Jeremiah 23:4 says, "'I will set up shepherds over them who will feed them; and they shall fear no more, nor be dismayed, nor shall they be lacking,' says the LORD." In other words, God is saying that when we are fed through the leaders He has set over us, we will no longer fear or be dismayed, and we will never lack again.

Satan's Strategy

Too often we get hung up on the humanity of the person we are intended to receive from. The Bible never said the vessel would be perfect. The gift of God inside the vessel is what is perfect.

When you have difficulty receiving from someone because you look at them in the natural, you risk losing out spiritually. When you have a problem receiving the Word from someone because they are black, white, female, male, too young, or too old, because you don't like their style or the way they say things, you're falling into a trap. The devil wants to keep you from receiving from the fivefold ministry gift in order to prevent the fullest measure of grace from coming into your life.

When the Word comes forth with the power of the anointing of the Holy Spirit and you're caught up in the flesh and judging the outward person, you're closing your spirit off from receiving a gift from God. In that word the fivefold minister is delivering is the grace to change your life.

The Principle of Impartation

There is a biblical principle of impartation. That means the gift inside the man or woman of God—the supernatural gift of Christ—is imparted into you.

Elijah was acknowledged as a great prophet. Elisha served him and worked alongside him. He knew Elijah had something great inside him—a supernatural gift of God—and when Elijah was about to be taken by the Lord, Elisha wanted to be sure he didn't miss out on what was available from him.

> And so it was, when they had crossed over, that Elijah said to Elisha, "Ask! What may I do for you, before I am taken away from you?" Elisha said, "Please let a double portion of your spirit be upon me." So he said, "You have asked a hard thing. Nevertheless, *if you see me when I am taken from you*, it shall be so for you; but if not, it shall not be so."
>
> —2 Kings 2:9–10, emphasis added

Elisha was indeed there when Elijah was taken up, and he did receive a supernatural impartation—a double portion of the anointing that was on Elijah's life. How did this happen? What was the condition for Elisha to receive the double portion? Elijah said, "If you see me when I am taken from you," then you will have what you ask for.

Elijah said to Elisha, "If you see *me*." He didn't say, "If you see the chariots." This phrase "if you see me" can actually mean, "If you see eye to eye with me." What Elijah was actually saying was, "Elisha, if you want what I have, then you've got to understand what I understand, and you have to see what I see in the spirit. When you understand what I understand and you see what I see, you will do more works than I've done."

The great Bible commentator Matthew Henry says this:

> Elijah promised him that which he asked, but under two provisos, v. 10. (1.) Provided he put a due value upon it and esteem it highly: this he teaches him to do by calling it a hard thing, not too hard for God to do, but too great for him to expect. Those are best prepared for spiritual blessings that are most sensible of their worth and their own unworthiness to receive them. (2.) Provided he kept close to his master, even to the last, and was observant of him: If thou see me when I am taken from thee, it shall be so, otherwise not. *A diligent attendance upon his master's instructions, and a careful observance of his example, particularly now in his last scene, were the condition and would be a proper means of obtaining much of his spirit.*[1]

Jesus said essentially the same thing to His followers: "Most assuredly, I say to you, he who believes in Me, the works that I do he will do also; and greater works than these he will do, because I go to My Father" (John 14:12).

The purpose of scriptural spiritual impartation is not simply to get what another person has; rather, the principle is that as you see eye to eye with them, understand what they understand, the result will be that you do more than they ever did.

The word *greater* in John 14:12 literally means more in number. The principle of impartation is that you are to receive from the apostle, prophet, evangelist, pastor, or teacher so you can understand what they understand and see things in the realm of the spirit the way they see them. When you do, you will always do greater works than they have done.

The Bible records that Elisha, who asked for a double portion, performed exactly twice as many miracles as Elijah. Actually when he died, he was one short, but when a dead man was thrown into Elisha's grave and landed on his bones, the man was raised from the dead.

> And it came to pass, as they were burying a man, that, behold, they spied a band of men; and they cast the man into the sepulchre of Elisha: and when the man was let down, and touched the bones of Elisha, he revived, and stood up on his feet.
>
> —2 KINGS 13:21, KJV

There was such a powerful impartation of God's power from Elijah to Elisha that God used even his dried-up, dead bones to heal.

The Double Portion—a Hard Thing

Do you want a double portion of the anointing on great men and women of God? I'm not necessarily talking about doing the same miracles. I'm talking about appropriating the same force that caused them to excel in what God called them to do and having it cause you to excel in what God has called you to do.

If so, learn from Elisha's example. He not only wanted the double portion of the anointing that Elijah had, but he was also willing to obey, humble himself, serve, and glean from Elijah's knowledge.

When Elisha asked to receive a double portion of Elijah's anointing, Elijah said, "You have asked a hard thing." Why did He say this? Because one of the hardest things for our natural minds to do is let go of our preprogrammed wrong thinking and wrong perspectives and take on, or appropriate, someone else's right thinking. This is because pride has such a stronghold on our natural minds, and it wants us to think we're already right. The hardest job of a fivefold ministry gift is not to teach the truth, but to break the stronghold of pride so that all the wrong thinking that is preprogrammed into our minds can be routed out.

> Elisha was willing to obey, humble himself, serve, and glean from Elijah's knowledge.

If all we as ministers ever do is to simply lay hands on people, there is really no meaningful impartation. Any impartation I can give that could bring the double portion anointing would come because someone seeks to understand what I understand and see things in the spirit realm the way I see them. A person must want a double-portion anointing enough to be willing to let the Holy Spirit change the way he or she thinks.

Receiving From the Gifts

When I accepted Christ, I pursued God with all my heart. I wanted to learn everything I could. I spent as much time listening to men of God as I could. In the first twelve weeks I was saved, I listened to more than sixty preaching tapes. I read the New Testament three times, and I was in a church service or Bible study of some sort five nights a week. I would have gone to church seven nights a week, but I couldn't find a service on the other two nights. So I would go over to some of my new Christian friends' houses, and we would worship God for hours together.

> A person must want a double-portion anointing enough to be willing to let the Holy Spirit change the way he or she thinks.

I had a brother in the Lord named Randy who spent a lot of time discipling me. He helped me through those emotional swings that most new converts go through. He taught me foundational scriptures that fortified me in the faith; even to this day those verses uphold me. Although I had many questions and didn't always agree with everything I was being taught, I still listened and respected the fact that he might know more than me.

I wanted to know the truth above everything. When I went to worship services, I latched on to every word the preacher said. It was an amazing season for me. Every week lightbulbs would go on in my head as I discovered new truths. In time I began to experience in my own life the things they were preaching about.

In my earliest days as a Christian I listened to an extended teaching series by evangelist Donnie Moore on the working of the Holy Spirit. What a message! I learned so much. I learned that God, by the Holy Spirit, could flow through me in supernatural power. I believed the word I was being taught, and as a result I was only four weeks old in the Lord when I started seeing God use me in the miraculous—and it has never ceased.

What happened to me as a young Christian? Was I an anomaly? Was I some freak? No. Having just been delivered from drug addiction, I passionately went after God. I opened my spirit to the grace gifts at work in others. And as I received the revelation that flowed through them, I gained favor that gave me access to the same power of God at work in their lives.

The worst thing I could have done would have been to maintain my pride and close my spirit to these leaders, these gifts from God. I would *not* have received the breakthroughs that I did, and I am convinced I would probably not be serving God today. Being open to the gift of God at work in others is just that serious. One of the worst things you can do is think you know better than someone who has more experience than you do. That's nothing but foolish pride, and pride comes before destruction.

If you are sitting under the pastor the Holy Spirit has led you to sit under, God has anointed him with a special ability to comprehend things you don't understand.

The purpose of that anointing is to show you how to live according to God's principles and how to use those principles for your own benefit and for God's glory. That's what the perfecting of the saints is all about.

Too Often We Won't Listen

Too often when the ministry gifts give counsel, we won't listen. We think they're just trying to hold us back or trying to get into our business. People of all ages have this tendency, because pride is something that constantly needs to be subdued in all of us. But for young believers, who have not learned the extent to which God will use fivefold ministers to help them grow, it's especially easy to cop an attitude with the pastor. What's worse, they may get other immature believers to jump on the bandwagon with them and say the pastor shouldn't tell anyone what they should or shouldn't do. But if that minister is the person God has placed as their spiritual authority, it is likely that He has anointed him to discern things in the spirit that those believers might never catch.

That pastor, like a parent, has been placed in that position to protect his congregation from things they may not yet understand. But if the members let pride tell them that they know what's best and that they can hear from God themselves and don't need any "pastor" to teach them, they should get ready, because they're going down. Proverbs 16:18 says, "Pride goes before destruction, and a haughty spirit before a fall."

Now I am not saying that everything a fivefold minister says is "thus saith the Lord." Unfortunately that is not the case. However, we need to recognize that God has placed revelation gifts inside the true fivefold minister for you and for me. If we close our spirits to them, we cannot receive what God has given to them for us.

Pride goes before destruction, and a haughty spirit before a fall. —Proverbs 16:18

I was attending a major Christian conference in 1989 when I overheard one of the conference ministers talk about the temper of one of the conference's main speakers. I was shocked because I had viewed this minister as a great man of God. When I attended his service the next day, I had great trouble receiving from Him.

The crowd was receiving a great breakthrough, but I didn't receive anything. All I kept thinking about was what I had heard the night before. The information about this man's character flaw caused me to close my spirit so I couldn't receive from the gift of God.

After that session the Holy Spirit showed me what I was doing, and I repented of my closed spirit. The rest of the conference was life-changing. Although I don't ever justify a person's sins or shortcomings, I have also learned that if I am waiting for the perfect preacher in order to receive from God, I will never receive anything.

Far too often Satan robs us of our ability to receive because we see the preacher's flaws. Again I am not talking about gross, vile sin. If you know a minister is struggling with flagrant immorality, you need to flee that person. If you know that a preacher—I don't care how famous or "anointed"—is an adulterer, drunk, crook, thief, or such like—*run!* Even if he has a genuine gift of revelation from heaven, if he has sold himself to slavery to the devil, he will drag down everyone around him.

Now we all have failings and shortcomings. We all have areas in our lives that God is working on. There is a difference between a blatant disregard for God's Word and the things He considers sin and missing the mark, as we all do. Too often the accuser will use the weaknesses we see in spiritual leaders to get us to close our spirits. It is a trap, but we fall into it for two main reasons.

The first is that we are afraid. We fear being mistreated or abused. We fear being let down or taken advantage of. So we withdraw from these ministers to whom God has given keys that will set us free. As a result, while we think we are protecting ourselves, we are actually solidifying our bondage.

The second main reason we close our spirits to the spiritual leaders God has put into our lives is pride expressed through a judgmental spirit. All judgmentalism is rooted in pride, and pride will always close your spirit to the gift of God. When you are full of pride, you can't see and hear, even when you think you can see and hear.

I discovered this truth in a new way in 2000. My staff and I were in a season of amazing visitation of the Holy Spirit. We were spending three to five hours a day in what we affectionately called "Holy Spirit times."

The Holy Spirit had called us to be with Him like never before. After nearly fifteen years of ministry I was holding the first church staff meetings in which the Holy Spirit truly was in charge. I had prayed for years for

God's guidance and control in our staff meetings, but we never really gave Him free rein. I don't think we even understood what that would look like.

We thought He was in control and that we were submitting to His leading, but on March 1, 2000, the Holy Spirit spoke. He said to me, "Why don't you invite Me to your staff meetings and give Me control?" I was shocked. We had been in revival for nearly a year, and we had seen more than a thousand people saved. For months we held services five nights a week with leaders from all over the area coming to receive a touch from God. We were known as the church where the Holy Spirit was in control. Yet the Holy Spirit wanted to take us to a whole new level.

I called all my staff together and told them what the Holy Spirit said. We then stood in a circle and truly invited the Holy Spirit to come and stand in our midst and take control. He came! We spent the next three hours repenting as He spoke to us about the many ways we grieve Him. This happened every day for weeks. He never talked with us about church business. He only spoke to us about heart business.

> Your pastor is a gift from God to you.

During this time of daily encounters with the Holy Spirit, He began to show us how much we had all been sitting on the judgment seat. I saw how much I had been doing that. What the Lord was showing me was so intense that after two weeks of the Holy Spirit revealing to me person after person and ministry after ministry I had judged, I cried out, "Is there anybody I haven't judged?"

As soon as I repented of being judgmental toward certain ministries, I started to notice something amazing. Whenever I would see those ministries on TV, I would find myself sitting in awe of the revelation knowledge God had given them. I had respected and even liked some of these ministries before, but I still had a level of judgment in my heart toward their teachings or their ministry methods. This judgment closed my spirit to receiving from them, even if just a little bit. When I repented, all of a sudden my spirit was open like never before to receive from the gift of Christ that was inside them.

This is why, no matter how old we are in the natural or how long we have known the Lord, it is important for us to keep a teachable spirit. When we are teachable, we keep ourselves open for the Lord to impart revelation into us through His ministry gifts. The process of impartation comes from being around someone who knows more than we know and understands more than we understand. This impartation requires that we come to the place where we see what they see and understand what they understand.

Treat Your Pastor as a Gift

Your pastor is a gift from God to you. God is using this gift to help you grow. He is giving you impartation through this gift. How then should you treat your pastor? As a gift.

How did Elisha come to the place where he saw eye to eye with Elijah, and understood what he understood and saw what he saw? Elisha served the man of God faithfully for seventeen years and treated him as a gift of God.

First Kings 19:21 says, "Then he set out to follow Elijah and became his attendant" (NIV). The word *attendant* here means Elisha was Elijah's "maid." Elisha's servant heart is the principle reason the anointing transferred from Elijah to him. Even the kings of the day understood this. They understood that when you have a right heart and spirit toward the gifts of God there comes a transfer of anointing.

> But Jehoshaphat asked, *"Is there no prophet of the LORD here*, that we may inquire of the LORD by him?" An officer of the king of Israel answered, "Elisha son of Shaphat is here. *He used to pour water on the hands of Elijah."* Jehoshaphat said, *"The word of the LORD is with him."*
>
> —2 KINGS 3:11–12, NIV, emphasis added

God puts people in your life who know more than you do about the things of the spirit to change your way of thinking.

When the king was looking for a prophet in the land after Elijah had died, one man stood up and said, "Yes, here is Elisha. And you want to know what his credentials are? He poured water on the hands of Elijah. Here is the man who was a servant to Elijah." And the king told his men to bring him that man, because if Elisha served the prophet of God, he had to have the prophet's anointing.

Do you want your pastor's anointing? Serve him. Treat him as a gift of God. He knows something you don't know and understands something you don't understand. And when you get around him, you will begin to see eye to eye with him. And when you see eye to eye with him, you'll begin to function in his anointing. That's the principle of impartation.

We live in a time when people say church leaders shouldn't tell the members what to do or not do. If I was a millionaire, you would let me teach you how to make money—in fact, you might pay me to teach you. Those in the fivefold ministry know something that's worth a whole lot more than a million dollars.

God puts people in your life who know more than you do about the things of the Spirit to change your way of thinking. If you're not living in the power that Jesus said you can live in and experiencing the victory the Word says you can have, if signs and wonders are not following you, if you're not overcoming all the power of the enemy, if you're still bound up in habitual sin, then something is wrong with your thinking.

There is a place called grace, and it comes through the knowledge of God. And God has given gifts to men and women—apostles, prophets, evangelists, pastors, and teachers. Why? The purpose is to change the way we think so we can grow in the favor of God. Then we can have access to the power of God for everything we need for life and godliness.

Chapter 6

ALL THINGS THAT PERTAIN TO LIFE

E VERYTHING WE NEED comes through grace. In 2 Peter 1 we read: "Grace and peace be multiplied unto you through the knowledge of God, and of Jesus our Lord, according as his divine power hath given unto us all things that pertain unto life and godliness" (vv. 2–3, KJV). Peter declares that God has given us access to all things that we need for life.

This powerful statement is confirmed throughout the Scriptures. God in His divine plan not only made a way for us to be saved, but through Christ's sacrifice He also provided the means for us to get all the things that we will ever need for life. Over and over again in Scripture God makes this promise to us.

> And my God shall supply all your need according to His riches in glory by Christ Jesus.
> —PHILIPPIANS 4:19

> But seek first the kingdom of God and His righteousness, and all these things shall be added to you.
> —MATTHEW 6:33

All the things we need for life include financial needs, emotional needs, relational needs, health needs, and wisdom. Through the revelation knowledge of God we can access the power of God to receive total provision in each of these areas of need. The reason so many Christians lack in these areas is because they lack revelation.

We live in a day when there are two major camps of teaching regarding God's intervention into man's financial affairs. The first camp believes that being poor somehow keeps you humble and thereby releases the grace and favor of God into your life. The other camp teaches that God wants you to enjoy the good life. They teach that it is God's will for you to have all the best that this life can offer: the best cars, finest clothes, nicest jewelry, and biggest homes.

The poor doctrine camp bases their beliefs on some biblical truths. They see throughout Scripture many warnings about the deceitfulness of riches and words of caution to the wealthy. They see how money has corrupted many good people throughout history. Their hallmark scriptures include:

> Then Jesus said to His disciples, "Assuredly, I say to you that it is hard for a rich man to enter the kingdom of heaven. And again I say to you, it is easier for a camel to go through the eye of a needle than for a rich man to enter the kingdom of God."
> —MATTHEW 19:23–24

> But those who desire to be rich fall into temptation and a snare, and into many foolish and harmful lusts which drown men in destruction

and perdition. For the love of money is a root of all kinds of evil, for which some have strayed from the faith in their greediness, and pierced themselves through with many sorrows.

—1 TIMOTHY 6:9–10

These are powerful passages of Scripture, and there are a multitude of others that support these truths. The poor doctrine camp, which has its roots in the ancient church, believes that the power of money to corrupt is so strong that the only way to avoid its influence is to live a life of lack. We see this manifest at varying degrees, from vows of poverty to simply rejecting that God would ever want to give us abundance.

On the other end of the spectrum is the prosperity camp. They too have many powerful scriptures to back them up. Here are just a couple:

Give, and it will be given to you: good measure, pressed down, shaken together, and running over will be put into your bosom. For with the same measure that you use, it will be measured back to you.

—LUKE 6:38

For assuredly, I say to you, whoever says to this mountain, "Be removed and be cast into the sea," and does not doubt in his heart, but believes that those things he says will be done, he will have whatever he says. Therefore I say to you, *whatever things you ask when you pray, believe that you receive them, and you will have them.*

—MARK 11:23–24,
emphasis added

67

These also are very powerful verses. Just as with the poor camp, there are a wide range of manifestations of the prosperity view—from God wants you rich and having the finest things in life to God's will is for the wealth of the wicked to be in the hands of God's people. Unfortunately, just as those on the poor doctrine side deny the prosperity scriptures, many on the prosperity side fail to heed the many, many warnings about the deceitfulness of riches. This refusal to acknowledge these verses and give them the same prominence the Bible does has led to many of the extremes we see in the prosperity message today.

A little later I will deal strongly with the bondage and weakness that the poverty doctrine has caused multitudes of Christians, but I want first to speak to the incredible abuses that are happening today on the prosperity side.

The Bible declares that judgment begins with the house of the Lord. God is going to judge the body of Christ, especially the leaders, who have surrendered themselves to the spirits of lust and greed. The Word of God makes this clear.

> But those who desire to be rich fall into temptation and a snare, and into many foolish and harmful lusts which drown men in destruction and perdition.
>
> —1 TIMOTHY 6:9,
> emphasis added

> For the love of money is a root of all kinds of evil, for which some have strayed from the faith in their

greediness, and pierced themselves through with many sorrows.

—1 TIMOTHY 6:10,
emphasis added

The Word of the Lord to many of today's leaders is Isaiah 56:11:

Yes, they are *greedy* dogs
Which never have enough.
And *they are shepherds*
Who cannot understand;
They all look to their own way,
Every one for his own gain,
From his own territory.

—Emphasis added

Not only are some of our leaders longing and lusting after wealth and are greedy for gain, but they also teach others to follow them in their indulgences and excesses, as Isaiah 56:12 declares:

"Come," one says, "I will bring wine,
And we will fill ourselves with intoxicating drink;
Tomorrow will be as today,
And much more abundant."

—Emphasis added

And we read in Ecclesiastes 5:10, "He that loveth silver shall not be satisfied with silver; *nor he that loveth abundance with increase*: this is also vanity" (KJV, emphasis added). Many leaders feed their insecurities and inferiorities with material things. They lust after money, manipulating Scripture and God's people to get what they want. They deceive themselves by believing they deserve an extravagant lifestyle because they are "anointed." While they should be protecting God's people from one of Satan's biggest traps, the deceitfulness of riches, they are instead leading the sheep to the slaughter.

The prophet Micah warned about this:

> Her heads judge for a bribe,
> *Her priests teach for pay,*
> *And her prophets divine for money.*
> Yet they lean on the LORD, and say,
> *"Is not the Lord among us?*
> *No harm can come upon us."*
> *Therefore because of you*
> *Zion shall be plowed* like a field.
>
> —MICAH 3:11–12,
> emphasis added

There are many fine, balanced leaders in the body of Christ. Unfortunately some of the most visible ones are also the ones guiltiest of these sins and abuses of the prosperity message. The lie that riches and natural wealth are the signs of God's favor and anointing on our lives has entrapped many of God's people.

> Many leaders feed their insecurities
> and inferiorities with material things.

We hide our bondage to the love of money under the guise of spiritual principles. We expend so much of our spiritual energy in the pursuit of the things of this world while heaven cries out for those who will "[love] not their lives unto death" (Rev. 12:11, KJV).

Many preachers today are more interested in the creature comforts of this life than the cross. Self-denial has become a burden too heavy to bear. "Give me wealth, power, and the finest the world has to offer" is their cry, while the saints of old look down from heaven wondering when "true ministry" will rise again within the church. We have lost our way!

Bondage of the Poor Doctrine

Even with the imbalances in prosperity teaching, the doctrine that being poor is godly has also done major damage to the body of Christ and the advancement of the gospel. Laity and leaders alike have felt guilty if they acquired any wealth. They think having wealth is somehow a betrayal of their faith. They were told that money will always lead to evil. Because of this they neither prayed for nor worked for financial abundance and advancement. They believe that those who desire more than what it takes to meet their most basic needs are somehow less pure and holy. They glorify their state of lack and make it a testament of their commitment to God.

All of these teachings are not only false doctrines, but they also border on idolatry and a works-oriented gospel. The belief that God, who gave us His own Son, desires for us to have just enough to survive is unscriptural, as the following verses attest.

> He who did not spare His own Son, but delivered
> Him up for us all, how shall He not with Him also
> freely give us all things?
>
> —Romans 8:32

> And my God shall supply all your need according
> to His riches in glory by Christ Jesus.
>
> —Philippians 4:19

The confusion has come because God has promised to meet all our needs, not to fulfill all of our lusts. The extreme prosperity camp thinks the things they lust for are what they need and what God wants them to have. The poor doctrine camp thinks that their need level is only what they must have to simply survive. Again both of these extremes are wrong.

Please notice that I have not said those who embrace the poverty doctrine have a poverty spirit. There is a poverty spirit at work behind the "Christians should be poor" doctrine, but a spirit of poverty is much more than that teaching alone. Let me explain.

What Is Your Real Need?

As I have traveled the nations, I have seen many wrong ways of thinking. None of them are more detrimental to the prosperity of God's people than what I call the "poverty mentality." Even in many of the most influential churches this poverty mentality has a stronghold. Even in churches that are considered faith ministries and that have received considerable teaching on the covenant of God, I find this poverty mentality pervasive.

In short, a poverty mentality is a willingness to accept

something less than God's best. It truly is very selfish to look only at God's provision from a self-serving, needs-oriented basis. The person with a poverty mentality thinks of material provision in terms of "what I need to get by." You've probably heard well-meaning saints say something like this: "All I need is a little food on my table, a small roof over my head, and some clothes on my back." This sounds well and good, but these well-meaning saints actually have bought into one of the greatest snow jobs the devil has ever pulled.

It may seem that someone who just wants what they need to get by has simply learned to be content in all circumstances. I would not for one moment disparage the apostle Paul's admonition that we learn to be content no matter what state we find ourselves in, but there is more to Paul's teaching than many realize.

> A poverty mentality is a willingness to accept something less than God's best.

In Philippians 4:11 Paul said, "Not that I speak in regard to need, for I have learned in whatever state I am, to be content." In that verse he was expressing the fact that because of his deep relationship with God, his spiritual contentment did not depend on his circumstances, on whether he was in prison or free. He was not stating that it is spiritual to accept less than all that God has for us. Paul was speaking about being in a place with God where, even if the circumstances were less than ideal, he could be totally content, emotionally and spiritually.

Never did he mean for these verses to be understood as admonishing God's people to live below God's covenant standards.

So many people in the church fail to understand that it is, and has always been, God's intention to bless His people. God's Word is replete with promises of total provision in all situations. Paul in Philippians 4:19 gave us the great truth, "My God shall supply all your needs according to His riches in glory." The Amplified Bible puts that verse this way: "And my God will liberally supply (fill to the full) your every need according to His riches in glory in Christ Jesus."

The Bible states that God will supply everything—that means every true need. If this is true, then what we need to discover is our true level of need. I would like to propose to you that your needs are much greater than you think.

Most Christians think their need is only what they must have in order to simply survive. That is not your true level of need. The Bible commands us to feed the hungry. How can you feed the hungry if you can barely feed yourself? The Bible also states that we are to clothe the naked. How can you clothe the naked if you have only enough money to buy clothes for yourself?

The Bible also commands us to go into all the world and preach the gospel. It costs a lot of money to preach the gospel. The gospel is free, but buying Bibles, airplane tickets, hotel rooms, and gas for your car, and keeping churches open and sound systems up to date all cost a lot of money.

Your need level is much greater than what you must have simply to survive. You need enough extra to help somebody else. We could take this much further, but I believe you are getting the point.

Even if you have enough money to pay your bills and have a little extra to help others, you still need more. The poverty mentality is willing to be satisfied with having the bare minimum. Your needs are not what you must have in order to survive. Your need level is what you must have in order to be most effective. Let me say that again: *your need level is what you must have in order to be most effective.*

So much of the church world is willing to live far beneath God's level of provision. In Philippians 4 God stated through the apostle Paul that He would completely supply all of our needs according to His riches. Think about that: He has riches.

We are the ones who set the standard at which we live. Let me explain what I mean. Back in the early nineties I was in San Diego, California, with a minister-friend of mine. I was in a hotel room and wanted to make a phone call. I was complaining about having to pay a fifty cent surcharge because I was using a calling card.

> Your need level is what you must have in order to be most effective.

My friend turned to me and asked, "What is the problem?" I replied, "What do you mean?" He then proceeded to tell me about a powerful principle God revealed to him several years earlier.

He began to share an incident that took place before

he entered full-time ministry when he used to run his own business. He was renting a large house at the time, and his income was very good. Then his business took a nosedive. He started to consider moving into a less expensive home. While he was praying, God spoke to him and said, "Son, I said I would meet all your needs. I didn't put a dollar limit on that. If your need level is seven hundred dollars a month, I will meet it. If it is seven thousand dollars a month, it makes no difference to Me. I have promised to meet *all your needs*. So whatever your need level is, I will meet it."

This revelation broke loose inside my life. At the time my wife was pregnant with our second child. We had been living in an apartment and were looking for a home to rent because the apartment was too small. We would be raising two children and running a ministry all out of our apartment, and we truly needed more space. We didn't need more space to survive. We could have survived in the apartment. But we really needed more space in order to be most effective.

After I returned home to Sacramento, California, my wife and I decided to take a step of faith and rent a house. Even though it was going to cost us a lot more money, we did it anyway. It was amazing. All the money we needed for the deposit and the rent each month miraculously came in. I didn't get a raise from my church. I can't really tell you where it came from even to this day. It just was there. God met our need.

It is not good enough to just survive. We only have a few years left before the return of Christ. We have to break free from this poverty mentality and start taking hold of everything that God has for us. It has never been

God's intention for His people to try to fulfill His purpose and plan here on the earth without having everything they truly need to be most effective.

Let us take this one step further. In 2 Corinthians 8:9 the Bible declares: "For you know the grace of our Lord Jesus Christ, that though He was rich, yet for your sakes He became poor, that you through His poverty might become rich." This verse tells us that Christ became poor. He took on our poverty so that we might gain His wealth.

The word *rich* in this scripture literally means wealthy or abounding in material goods. Christ died to free us from the spirit of poverty. God is not poor, nor does He embrace or accept a poverty mentality.

In Psalm 84:11 the Bible declares: "For the LORD God is a sun and shield; the LORD bestows favor and honor; no good thing does he withhold from those whose walk is blameless" (NIV). The psalmist David declares in this verse that God would withhold nothing from those who serve Him. Never in Scripture do we see God exalting, promoting, or encouraging His people to remain bound in their poverty.

As we have already discussed, a poverty mentality is about much more than money. It is the willingness to accept something far less than God's best. We need to become a people who not only believe God wants to bless us, but we also need to learn how to tap into the total provision of God for our lives on a daily basis, receiving all that we truly need in order to be most effective.

Let me give you an example. As I have traveled the nations of the world, I have learned some very important lessons. When I first started traveling, I used to take what I called the economy route. I would stay in one of the least expensive hotels, eat at the cheapest fast-food restaurants, and generally do without. I thought that I was being a good steward of God's money by doing this. We really didn't have a lot, so I tried to make the money we had go as far as it could.

As I had the opportunity to spend time with men of God who had been traveling internationally much longer than I had, I was told repeatedly that I needed to stop traveling so cheaply. They explained that I wasn't really being a good steward with all that God had given to me when I stayed in inexpensive hotels and ate fast food.

They said the most important part of my traveling was the time I spent ministering. Often I would minister two or three times a day, spending many hours preaching and praying for people. They explained to me that if I wasn't getting the proper rest and eating correctly, it would affect my preaching.

Many of these less expensive hotels had poor mattresses, no support services, and could be very uncomfortable overall. After hearing them out, I realized that in order to be most effective in my preaching, I needed to stay in places that had adequate facilities. I thought I was being a good steward of the ministry's finances by cutting corners, but in the end I realized that being so thrifty was causing me to be a bad steward of my calling.

After hearing this same counsel on several occasions, I decided to take a step of faith. I used to return from these trips exhausted because I never really slept or rested very well. But then I started paying the extra money to stay in better hotels. I told God that I needed Him to supply the difference.

What happened was amazing. As soon as I gave my need to Him, the money to pay the larger hotel bills was there. The poverty mentality that was on my life caused me to think in the smallest terms and to cut corners where they should not be cut. I am not saying that we should not be wise with our money. We should be very wise. But we should not be afraid to spend money that is needed to help us to be *most* effective in what God has called us to do.

> Ye have not, because ye ask not.
> —James 4:2, KJV

I am not talking about giving yourself a license to lust for extravagant things. I am talking about asking God to supply what it takes for you to be most effective in fulfilling the purposes of God.

I don't stay in three-thousand-dollar suites, nor do I stay in nineteen-dollar motels. God used those men of God to set me free from my limited thinking that caused me to believe I could help God out financially. God does not need our help. He needs our obedience. God is more than able to fully provide for all our needs. The reason most of us live so far below our most effective level is because we have never truly asked God for more than what we have. Most of us settle for less than God's best. The Bible says, "Ye have not, because ye ask not" (James 4:2, KJV).

The poverty mentality will keep you from tapping into the grace of God, which has freely given you all things.

Grace is the favor of God that has given us access to the power of God for *all* things that pertain to *life* and godliness. At the beginning of this chapter I said that God's grace provides us with all the things that we need for life. These include financial needs, emotional needs, relational needs, health needs, and wisdom. We have looked at financial needs. Let's now look briefly at these other areas of need.

Emotional Needs

We all have emotional needs. God made us emotional beings. For far too long the church taught us to ignore our feelings instead of understanding what causes them. They made it seem as though we wouldn't feel anxious or angry or sad if we just had enough faith. So we tried to deny what we felt, but those emotions seemed to come up again and again.

Our emotions are a powerful force in our lives. Scientists say that up to 70 percent of our strength and energy comes from our emotions.[1] Our emotions give us the energy and power to accomplish things, whether they are good or bad things.

If our emotional needs aren't met, we will often look to ungodly and unholy things to try to meet them. For instance, we have an emotional need for joy. We need that joy to give us strength and health. If we don't find joy in our relationship with God, we will often seek for it in the world. Some look for it in entertainment, others in parties and riotous living, still others in alcohol and drugs. Some think building up wealth, shopping, or food will bring them joy.

Those things may make us feel a little better for a

while, but they will not bring true joy. Scripture says the "joy of the LORD is your strength" (Neh. 8:10). When you enter into the place called grace and behold the Lord as He is, you will find a joy so deep that it will cause you to never again look to the things of this world to meet that emotional need.

God is the only one who can truly satisfy our emotional needs. We have an emotional need for peace, which is why Jesus said, "Peace I leave with you, My peace I give to you; not as the world gives do I give to you. Let not your heart be troubled, neither let it be afraid" (John 14:27).

We also have an emotional need for love, which is why the Holy Spirit inspired the apostle Paul to write that "hope does not disappoint, because the love of God has been poured out in our hearts by the Holy Spirit who was given to us" (Rom. 5:5). God and God alone can meet all of our emotional needs—and the good news is that *He wants to meet them.*

Relational Needs

One of the most devastating areas of emotional lack is loneliness. Because of loneliness many Christians have entered into relationships that are unhealthy and often unholy.

God knows that we have needs for companionship. He has promised to supply all of our needs, but that doesn't necessarily mean He will meet that need by sending us a boyfriend, girlfriend, or spouse. God has given us the opportunity to have a relationship with Him that can be more emotionally satisfying than any companionship here on the earth. We must realize the incredible access

He has given us. Grace is the favor of God that gives us access to the power of God. However, as we have learned, we only get that access when we have revelation.

When I first got saved, I made one of the greatest decisions of my life. I told God that I would not date. I told Him that I had messed up every relationship I'd ever had and that I was going to wait on Him to lead me to the right person if that was His will. When I accepted Christ, I had such an incredible encounter with God that I became convinced He was the only companion I would ever need. I believed that He could satisfy.

Over the next few years I developed such a deep, intimate relationship with God that I didn't care if I ever got married. I would spend hours walking, talking, and sitting with God, just enjoying His presence. He taught me how to pursue Him. I had learned to be so content in Him that I *never* got lonely. Even now when I am on the road for weeks by myself, I never get lonely, because He is ever present.

After more than three years God brought to me my incredible wife. She is truly a gift from heaven. We have been married for more than twenty-three years, and we have never had a fight. We have never exchanged harsh words or raised our voices to each other. I believe the main reason for this is that we have both learned to let God meet our emotional needs. We, therefore, are not "needy" for each other. We don't drain the life from each other because of our need for companionship. We release life to each other because we are already full and complete in Him.

Health Needs

The Bible tells us that it is God's desire that we be in good health (3 John 2). Yet many people deal with sickness at some point in their lives. They may be facing a common cold or a chronic illness, but no matter what the situation, Scripture is clear that God is in the healing business:

> But He was wounded for our transgressions, He was bruised for our iniquities; the chastisement for our peace was upon Him, *and by His stripes we are healed.*
>
> —Isaiah 53:5,
> emphasis added

> Is anyone among you sick? Let him call for the elders of the church, and let them pray over him, anointing him with oil in the name of the Lord *And the prayer of faith will save the sick, and the Lord will raise him up.*
>
> —James 5:14–15,
> emphasis added

> Who Himself bore our sins in His own body on the tree, that we, having died to sins, might live for righteousness—*by whose stripes you were healed.*
>
> —1 Peter 2:24,
> emphasis added

The Bible makes it plain that God wants to heal our bodies. But He is not only in the healing business—He is also in the business of keeping us healthy. In January of 2001 I was at home watching Jesse Duplantis preaching on television. He was sharing about how when he first read Isaiah 55:3, he became convinced that Jesus had paid the price so we didn't have to get sick anymore.

When Jesse as a young believer told his pastor about this revelation, his pastor almost tried to change his mind. Jesse, however, saw this in the Word and began to declare, "I ain't getting sick no more."

His pastor was concerned that if Jesse did get sick, he would become discouraged and his young faith might be shaken. Isn't it amazing that instead of encouraging young believers to trust God's Word with all their hearts, those of us who are older in the Lord sometimes teach them through our unbelief that God doesn't do what He said He would do? God forgive us for propagating fear and unbelief under the guise of protecting the young in faith.

By this time I was watching Jesse share this story, I had flown well over a million miles around the world, had seen amazing miracles in my own meetings, and watched as God had saved and delivered hundreds of thousands. However, I would get a cold or flu three or four times a year. My kids would get sick at school, they would give it to me, and I would then give it back to them. We believed in sowing and reaping.

On this January day watching Brother Jesse changed my life. I had always believed in the healing power of God, and I believed God could keep us healthy. Even though I had experienced God's healing touch, I hadn't entered into the place where I walked in divine health. This day changed all that. As Jesse spoke, my spiritual eyes were opened to a new dimension. All of a sudden I saw by revelation that I had the legal right to access the power of God in order to walk in divine health. I had always believed it, but now I *saw* it!

That revelation gave me the grace—the access to the power of God for all I needed—to walk in supernatural health. I stood up in my house and declared, "I'm not getting sick anymore." I then stood up in service after service and declared, "I don't get sick anymore. Divine health is flowing through my body."

Since that day I have not been sick one time. It wasn't the confession that produced the faith to bring the miracle to pass. It was the revelation that produced the faith that caused me to boldly confess the promises of God. It has been twelve years, and I don't get sick anymore.

Remember back in chapter 2 when we talked about the sower and the seed, and how when the Word comes it is tested and tried. I had heard and even preached about God's divine health. However, whenever I would feel those first few signs of sickness, I would surrender. I would begin to say, "I feel a cold coming on." And lo and behold, I would get sick.

The Word of revelation had tried for years to bear fruit in my life, so that I would access the power of God to walk in divine health, but the seed of that revelation had no root and died the moment the first cold symptoms appeared. Sometimes I would expect to get sick even before any symptoms appeared because everybody else in my house was sick.

After this revelation truly broke loose inside me, I no longer surrender to sickness. In the twelve years I've been walking in divine health, I have on a few occasions felt the very first signs of a cold trying to come on. I would hear a voice in my head say, "Well, it's going to happen this time. It's been a good run, but this time you're going to get sick."

In those moments the Word in my heart was under assault. Fortunately I had learned to fight for this truth. I would immediately begin to declare, "I don't get sick anymore. Divine health is flowing through my body."

I kid you not—*every time* the symptoms would flee, and I would not get sick. I had received enough revelation so that I had the grace/favor needed to access the power of God to walk in the health that Jesus's stripes had purchased. This is not just for me. The same divine health I have walked in is available to *every* believer.

Wisdom

James 1:5–8 tells us, "If any of you lacks wisdom, let him ask of God, who gives to all liberally and without reproach, and it will be given to him. But let him ask in faith, with no doubting, for he who doubts is like a wave of the sea driven and tossed by the wind. For let not that man suppose that he will receive anything from the Lord; he is a double-minded man, unstable in all his ways."

God wants His people to have His wisdom. Scripture says:

> And I have filled him with the Spirit of God, in wisdom, in understanding, in knowledge, and in all manner of workmanship.
>
> —Exodus 31:3

> But where can wisdom be found?
> And where is the place of understanding?...

From where then does wisdom come?
And where is the place of understanding?
It is hidden from the eyes of all living,
And concealed from the birds of the air.
Destruction and Death say,
"We have heard a report about it with our ears."
God understands its way,
And He knows its place....
Then He saw wisdom and declared it;
He prepared it, indeed, He searched it out.
And to man He said,
"Behold, the fear of the Lord, that is wisdom,
And to depart from evil is understanding."
—Job 28:12, 20–23, 27–28

Not only does God desire that His people have His wisdom, He wants to reveal His wisdom through the church. Ephesians 3:10 says, "To the intent that now *the manifold wisdom of God* might *be made known by the church* to the principalities and powers in the heavenly places" (emphasis added).

It doesn't matter what your background is—whether you're young or old, rich or poor. God will freely give His wisdom to those who ask and believe for it. God has given you and me access through grace by the revelation knowledge of Him to all things we need for life and godliness, and that includes accessing the wisdom of God.

God has made a way for us to access everything we will ever need for life. He makes provisions to meet our needs and cause us to be most effective in serving Him. He has done this by giving us His grace, which is the favor of God that gives us access to the power of God for all things pertaining to life and godliness. We have looked at how He gives us access to all things pertaining to life. Now let's see how He gives us access to all things pertaining to godliness.

Chapter 7

ALL THINGS THAT PERTAIN TO GODLINESS

L ET'S LOOK AGAIN at our key passage from 2 Peter:

> Grace and peace be multiplied to you in the knowl-
> edge of God and of Jesus our Lord, as *His divine
> power has given to us all things* that pertain to life
> and *godliness*, through the knowledge of Him who
> called us by glory and virtue, by which have been
> given to us exceedingly great and precious prom-
> ises, *that through these you may be partakers of the
> divine nature, having escaped the corruption that
> is in the world through lust.*
>
> —2 PETER 1:2–4,
> emphasis added

In the mid-1990s I was visiting the church of a very
famous minister. This pastor had built two megachurches
and was known as a major apostolic voice to the nations.
I was in the service during worship, standing in one of
the side wings, when I saw an open vision.

Suddenly I saw the sanctuary with this pastor on the
stage preaching. Above the crowd was the manifested

glory of God. The people filled every seat, and lines of people were marching into the church for as far as the eye could see. Beneath the first 40 percent of those in the sanctuary was a thick stone foundation. It was about four to five feet thick. But the foundation quickly receded the farther back I looked. It rapidly became paper thin with large holes everywhere.

Below all the people I saw a huge demon spirit. It was the spirit of religion. It would open its mouth, speak, and a black vapor would come out and rise up to cover the eyes of those in the back 60 percent of the sanctuary. The vapor couldn't touch the people with the stone foundation.

> The spirit of religion called the
> spirit of holiness "religious."

When this vapor would cover the eyes of these people, they would raise their hands and shout "Hallelujah," because they thought they were free. Then they would blindly walk forward to one of the areas where there was a hole in the foundation, and the demon spirit would reach up and pull them down.

Nobody would notice, though, because another person would walk in the back door to fill the person's space. In my vision this demon of religion opened his mouth and spoke, and when he did he called the spirit of holiness "religious."

I had no idea at that time what was truly going on in that church. I was deeply troubled by this vision.

Through this vision God not only was revealing to me what was going on at that church, but He also showed me some powerful truths for the body of Christ at large.

What Is a Religious Spirit?

The term *religious spirit* has been thrown around in recent years like a Frisbee. We often use this term to attack those we disagree with. We accuse them of being "religious" in an attempt to keep them from hindering us from walking in our perceived freedom.

If a church or minister is liturgical in his approach, we call it religious. If a minister preaches any form of holiness that conflicts with our lifestyles, we call it religious. When the church world began to embrace a secular approach to evangelism and church growth based on business principles, if you spoke up against it you were called religious. When you go to a "Christian" youth concert and those on the platform are half-dressed, covered with tattoos, and thrashing around as if practicing some hedonistic ritual, if you dare question the spirituality of this event, you are called religious.

We have learned to use attacking words to bully our critics into silence. The homosexuals call those who speak against their lifestyle "homophobic." The "Christians" who want to live a loose, unholy, worldly lifestyle all in the name of Jesus call their critics "religious." This started primarily during the antiestablishment movements of the sixties and seventies. It was promoted by the Christian rock music industry to silence the many pastors who were concerned about embracing the sounds and look of the world. Many fine ministers who had deep spiritual concerns were shouted down as being religious and out of touch with the young generation.

> The church rebelled against legalism
> but ran headlong into lawlessness.

This trend toward calling everyone religious was also an overreaction to the very damaging effects of legalism. Legalism placed people in a bondage to outward acts of "holiness" without giving them the power to live holy. As a result, God's people lived life full of guilt and turmoil, never having the power to overcome sin and yet always bound by its influence in their lives.

God doesn't want us to live in legalism. But He also doesn't want us to reject the truth by denouncing it as "religious." This is why we must get a revelation about the religious spirit.

A religious spirit has *two* faces, not just one. It has the face of legalism with which most of us are acquainted, but it also has another face—the face of lawlessness. The church rebelled against legalism but ran headlong into lawlessness. They thought they were free when they dumped legalism, but many simply switched to the other side of a religious spirit.

Legalism Is the Opposite of Grace

The first face of a religious spirit is the face of legalism. There is much misunderstanding about this term. *Legalism* is the reliance upon the works of man to gain access to and favor with God. It is the opposite of grace, which is the undeserved favor of God that gives us access to the power of God for everything we need for life and godliness.

True legalism is manifested when we lean upon our good works in order to gain God's favor. We saw this in the Galatian church. They started out trusting in God's grace but tried to gain further favor with God by encouraging men to get circumcised. They were returning to the requirements of the Law in order to gain access to God.

This same sin has been committed throughout church history. We try to gain access to the favor of God through what we do, when in reality we are supposed to do good things because we already have access to God. In our day, though, legalism has taken on an additional meaning.

Legalism also applies to requirements placed upon the saints, usually by the clergy, that are supposed to be evidence of a consecrated, God-fearing life. Often these requirements cause people to feel condemned and guilt-ridden, because they are told that if they fail to live up to these man-made standards, they will go to hell.

This area gets a little tricky because much of what these preachers of holiness are saying has validity. But often the application of the principles will bring people into bondage instead of freedom. In these cases the legalistic acts are usually based upon true, biblical principles, but they are taken to extremes and presented as issues that could send a person to hell. As I said, many of these areas of "holiness" are genuine and worth being addressed, but they are often maturity issues rather than problems that could determine where a person will spend eternity.

For example, many churches used to preach that it was a sin to go to the movies. The fact is that it is sinful to go to *some* movies. Some movies contain the kinds of things Scripture tells us to flee:

> I will set nothing wicked before my eyes.
>
> —PSALM 101:3

> Then He said to them, "Take heed what you hear."
>
> —MARK 4:24

> Flee also youthful lusts; but pursue righteousness, faith, love, peace with those who call on the Lord out of a pure heart.
>
> —2 TIMOTHY 2:22

> But *fornication* and *all uncleanness* or covetousness, let it not even be named among you, as is fitting for saints; neither filthiness, nor *foolish talking, nor coarse jesting, which are not fitting*, but rather giving of thanks. For this you know, that no fornicator, unclean person, nor covetous man, who is an idolater, has any inheritance in the kingdom of Christ and God. Let no one deceive you with empty words, for because of these things the wrath of God comes upon the sons of disobedience. *Therefore do not be partakers with them.*
>
> —EPHESIANS 5:3–7,
> emphasis added

Have we not become partakers when we pay money to sit and watch sinful acts being committed and allow ourselves to be entertained by such? We, by our complicity and our financial support of such movies and TV programs, have empowered these sins to continue, and thus we too have become guilty of the very sins ourselves.

Many pastors were deeply concerned about the influence of ungodly movies and music on their congregations and preached against them. Unfortunately, as the body of Christ is notorious for doing, we went to extremes. We labeled all movies and all TV shows as "of the devil." In order to get our congregations to stay away from them, we used the old tactic of fear. We took genuine truth and put the "you'll go to hell if you do this!" label on it.

The fact is that there are some movies and TV programs that Christians have no business watching. But just because a Christian saw the movie or TV show doesn't mean he has lost his salvation.

Another area that fell under the banner of legalism was clothing and makeup. Once again there are true, biblical principles at the root here, but often the application has been flawed. First Timothy 2:9 says, "In like manner also, that the women adorn themselves in modest apparel, with propriety and moderation, not with braided hair or gold or pearls or costly clothing."

In this verse Paul was revealing a truth to us. We are to shine forth our inward beauty and not be caught up in the fashions of our day. We are not to follow the world's trends. We are to do all things with modesty and moderation. However, this too was taken to an extreme. Women were told that if they wore makeup, pants, or skirts that were above their ankles they were "going to hell."

The fact is, we as Christians, both men and women, need to walk in modesty and moderation. Today many have gone the other direction. We see twelve-year-old girls coming to church dressed like their favorite scantily clad pop star, teenage guys dressed like thugs, and others dressed like the most extreme elements of our society.

They claim they are free in Christ, but the reality is they are still bound by a love for the world. We read in James 4:4: "Adulterers and adulteresses! Do you not know that friendship with the world is enmity with God? Whoever therefore wants to be a friend of the world makes himself an enemy of God."

I am not talking about the unsaved people who walk into our churches. The Bible doesn't say they must change their clothes in order to get right with God. That is legalism. But once they are a part of the household of faith, people *must* be taught that the Christian is to be modest and live in moderation. We are not to be given to the love and lust of the world. We must walk circumspectly before our God.

Lawlessness—Just Another Form of Bondage

Because of the extremes in our teaching about holiness, many Christians and pastors ran to the other face of the religious spirit, which is lawlessness. Instead of seeking a balanced view, Christians, including ministers, will watch all sorts of R-rated movies and vile TV programs. They will wear just about anything—or not wear enough. They will even embrace aspects of the culture that are extreme and promote ungodliness.

They justify this by saying, "I am free in Christ to do all these things." Yet, just as with legalism, this too is bondage and deception. God wants us to live godly and holy—not to earn His favor but because of it.

Under this new expression of a religious spirit, lawlessness has become "spiritual." It is the "enlightened" Christian who walks in his God-given freedom and engages the spirit of the age. Preachers—prominent ones—sit around boozing it up, using foul language, womanizing, and engaging in all sorts of sin. I have personally heard and seen them say, "We are under grace, not the law. We are free to do these things. Look at how anointed I am. God has given me a special grace."

When I have confronted them, they have called me "religious." The drunken parties, orgies, drug use, stealing, and more that goes on within some ministry circles would shock you. The spirit of lawlessness that is loose in the church today is a product of the spirit of religion. All of this has been allowed to fester because the church has failed to understand what grace truly is and how it works.

> God wants us to live godly and holy—not to earn His favor but because of it.

Legalism bypassed the undeserved nature of grace and used fear to influence people's behavior. Those who embraced lawlessness misinterpreted grace as a license to live without accountability.

Grace is the favor of God that gives us access to the power of God for all things we need for life *and godliness*. Through grace we can live godly. Through grace we can access the power we need to overcome the lust of the flesh, the lust of the eyes, and the pride of life.

Through the revelation knowledge of God we can access this power to walk in holiness.

> Therefore gird up the loins of your mind, be sober, and *rest your hope fully upon the grace that is to be brought to you at the revelation of Jesus Christ*; as obedient children, not conforming yourselves to the former lusts, as in your ignorance; but as He who called you is holy, you also be holy in all your conduct, because it is written, *"Be holy, for I am holy."*
> —1 PETER 1:13–16,
> emphasis added

We can live a God-like, God-pleasing life. It is not impossible. Although our access to God is based upon His unmerited favor, we still can please or displease Him through our actions, as the following verses attest:

> But do not forget to do good and to share, for with such sacrifices God is well *pleased.*
> —HEBREWS 13:16,
> emphasis added

> But when Jesus saw it, He was greatly *displeased* and said to them, "Let the little children come to Me, and do not forbid them; for of such is the kingdom of God."
> —MARK 10:14,
> emphasis added

God has called us to live in such a way that our lives are pleasing to Him. We can do this only by His power, which has come to us through the revelation knowledge of Him—the revelation that the power of sin has been broken over our lives and that we have access to the power of God to live holy.

The Power of Sin Is Broken

Before grace, we were bound. The Law couldn't deliver us from the power of sin, but Christ broke that power when He died on the cross. Romans 8:3 says, "For God has done what the Law could not do, [its power] being weakened by the flesh [the entire nature of man without the Holy Spirit]. Sending His own Son in the guise of sinful flesh and as an offering for sin, *[God] condemned sin in the flesh [subdued, overcame, deprived it of its power over all who accept that sacrifice]*" (AMP, emphasis added).

The apostle Paul also says in Romans 6:14, "For sin shall not have dominion over you, for you are not under law but under grace." Because you are under the favor of God that has given you access to the power of God, you now have the power to overcome sin.

When He died on the cross, Christ subdued and overcame the power of sin, so now through the power of the Holy Spirit we too can subdue and overcome the flesh. For years ministers preached that as long as we are "in the flesh"—that is, in this natural body—we cannot walk free from sin. This doctrine, though common, is contrary to the clear teachings of the New Testament. Consider the following verses:

> Jesus answered them, "Most assuredly, I say to you, whoever commits sin is a slave of sin. And a slave does not abide in the house forever, but a son

abides forever. *Therefore if the Son makes you free, you shall be free indeed.*"

—JOHN 8:34–36,
emphasis added

Whoever has been born of God does not sin, for His seed remains in him; and he cannot sin, because he has been born of God.

—1 JOHN 3:9,
emphasis added

We know that *whoever is born of God does not sin; but he who has been born of God keeps himself, and the wicked one does not touch him.*

—1 JOHN 5:18,
emphasis added

Therefore *do not let sin reign in your mortal body,* that you should obey it in its lusts. And do not present your members as instruments of unrighteousness to sin, but present yourselves to God as being alive from the dead, and your members as instruments of righteousness to God. *For sin shall not have dominion over you, for you are not under law but under grace.*

—ROMANS 6:12–14,
emphasis added

For the law of the Spirit of life in *Christ Jesus has made me free from the law of sin and death.*

—ROMANS 8:2,
emphasis added

But if you are led by the Spirit, you are not under the law. Now the works of the flesh are evident, which are: adultery, fornication, uncleanness, lewdness, idolatry, sorcery, hatred, contentions, jealousies, outbursts of wrath, selfish ambitions, dissensions, heresies, envy, murders, drunkenness, revelries, and the like; of which I tell you beforehand, just as I also told you in time past, that those who practice such things will not inherit the kingdom of God. But the fruit of the Spirit is love, joy, peace, long-suffering, kindness, goodness, faithfulness, gentleness, self-control. Against such there is no law. *And those who are Christ's have crucified the flesh with its passions and desires.* If we live in the Spirit, let us also walk in the Spirit.

—Galatians 5:18–25,
emphasis added

For *the grace of God* that brings salvation has appeared to all men, *teaching us that,* denying ungodliness and worldly lusts, *we should live soberly, righteously, and godly in the present age,* looking for the blessed hope and glorious appearing of our great God and Savior Jesus Christ, who gave Himself for us, *that He might redeem us from every lawless deed* and purify for Himself His own special people, zealous for good works.

—Titus 2:11–14,
emphasis added

There are many, many more verses along the same lines. In the face of such overwhelming evidence in Scripture, we can draw only one conclusion. God has called us through His grace to live a holy, godly life. The reason most Christians don't rise to this level of freedom and holy living is that we are not accessing the power of God to do so.

Grace is the favor of God that gives us access to the power of God. This access is increased only as we grow in the revelation knowledge of God. That is why the Scriptures say, "My people are destroyed for lack of knowledge" (Hosea 4:6). When we lack the revelation knowledge of God, we lack the access to the power to live a godly life.

> God has called us through His
> grace to live a holy, godly life.

God has provided all things that we need to live godly and to become more like Christ through the revelation knowledge of Him. As the apostle Paul wrote:

> And all of us, as with unveiled face, [because we] continued to behold [in the Word of God] as in a mirror the glory of the Lord, are constantly being transfigured into His very own image in ever increasing splendor and from one degree of glory to another; [for this comes] from the Lord [Who is] the Spirit.
> —2 CORINTHIANS 3:18, AMP

As we enter into the place called grace and behold the glory of the Lord, we are being transformed into the *godly* image of Jesus.

Chapter 8

SETTING THE RECORD STRAIGHT

I HAVE BEEN AMAZED at the recent flood tide of a new teaching about grace. This popular message is much different from the gospel that has been preached during every recorded revival in history. From the days of John Wesley, Jonathan Edwards, Charles Finney, George Whitefield, and down through the ages, great moves of God have always been marked by cries of repentance and conviction of sin. Although revival leaders throughout history have differed on some doctrinal points, they all preached that God's people must live a holy life marked by repentance. Their revivals were filled with cries of brokenness and godly sorrow not only from the lost but also from many professing Christians and ministers. People were called to separate from the world and to abhor sin.

That's because a true revival does two things. First, it causes the church to turn away from her backsliding, and second, it causes men and women to turn to Christ. Revival always includes the conviction of sin on the part of the church. And there is always a message of brokenness and godly sorrow, not one that says the Holy Spirit won't convict us of sin, as some of these modern grace teachers claim. It is as evangelist Billy Sunday once said, "What a spell the devil seems to cast over the church today!"[1]

Conviction and repentance cannot be separated from revival. To quote revivalist Charles Finney, "Revival is a renewed conviction of sin and repentance, followed by an intense desire to live in obedience to God. It is giving up one's will to God in deep humility."[2] The great evangelist and theologian John Wesley said those who do great things for God shun sin. He once wrote, "Give me one hundred preachers who fear nothing but sin and desire nothing but God, and I care not whether they be clergymen or laymen, they alone will shake the gates of Hell and set up the kingdom of Heaven upon Earth."[3] Look also at what preacher Charles Spurgeon had to say about repentance in the life of the believer:

> Repentance and forgiveness are riveted together by the eternal purpose of God. What God has joined together let no man put asunder. Repentance must go with remission, and you will see that it is so if you think a little upon the matter. It cannot be that pardon of sin should be given to an impenitent sinner; this would only confirm him in his evil ways and teach him to think little of evil. If the Lord were to say, "You love sin and live in it, and you are going on from bad to worse, but all the same, I forgive you," this would proclaim a horrible license for iniquity.... That is not a true repentance which does not come of faith in Jesus, and that is not true faith in Jesus which is not tinctured with

Setting the Record Straight

repentance. Faith and repentance, like Siamese twins, are vitally joined together....Faith and repentance are but two spokes in the same wheel, two handles of the same plough. Repentance has been well described as a heart broken for sin, and from sin....It is a change of mind of the most thorough and radical sort.[4]

Today you hardly hear those kinds of messages. They have been replaced with a teaching that says, "Your sins are all forgiven, so don't worry about how you live. If someone tells you to change your behavior, they are putting you under the law not grace. There is no need to feel bad about what you're doing. Jesus loves you. He did all the work, and you just need to believe He paid the price for your sins."

In every effective deception there is some truth, and that is the case with the false grace message that is sweeping the world today. That is why we must rightly divide the Word to see what God has to say about grace, forgiveness, repentance, and sin. I want to spend this chapter tackling the hard questions head-on:

- Do we have to obey Jesus's teachings?

- What is the role of the Law in the season of grace?

- Does the Holy Spirit convict Christians of sin?

- Are Christians required to repent?

I may have ruffled a few feathers in the last chapter, but I am sure to step on some toes in this one. I am not out to attack anyone. My heart is simply to separate the truth about grace from the error, because that is the only way the body of Christ can grow and be set free from bondage and be victorious over sin. So let's dive right in.

Do We Have to Obey Jesus's Teachings?

There is a shocking and very dangerous teaching by a few popular ministers today that Jesus sometimes spoke of things that were part of the old covenant and at other times He spoke of things that were under the new covenant. They claim that until His resurrection Jesus was preaching the Law and therefore we don't have to obey those teachings. This is probably one of the most dangerous and deceptive doctrines out there today, so let's allow the Word to clarify this issue.

We read in Luke 16:16, "The law and the prophets were until John. Since that time the kingdom of God has been preached, and everyone is pressing into it." So Jesus says the Law was only until John the Baptist. Once John the Baptist started preaching His message of repentance, the new era of the kingdom of God—the new covenant—started.

We see elsewhere in Scripture that Jesus came preaching the kingdom of heaven, not the Old Testament law:

> From that time Jesus began to preach and to say, "Repent, for the kingdom of heaven is at hand."
> —MATTHEW 4:17

But He said to them, "I must preach the kingdom of God to the other cities also, because for this purpose I have been sent."

—Luke 4:43

Now some erroneously claim that the apostle Paul preached the gospel of grace and that his message was different from what John the Baptist and Jesus taught. This is not only false—it's dangerous. Those who make this claim have exalted Paul above Jesus. And they are just plain wrong when they say Jesus preached about the coming kingdom of God while Paul preached a message of grace.

Scripture says, "Then Paul dwelt two whole years in his own rented house, and received all who came to him, *preaching the kingdom of God and teaching the things which concern the Lord Jesus Christ* with all confidence, no one forbidding him" (Acts. 28:30–31, emphasis added). Paul was "preaching the kingdom of God and teaching the things which concern the Lord Jesus Christ." In other words, he was preaching the same message of the kingdom that Jesus taught.

All doctrine we embrace *must* be filtered through the teachings of Christ. Jesus came to proclaim the *new* message of grace. The new message is what gives life.

Jesus said, "The thief does not come except to steal, and to kill, and to destroy. I have come that they may have life, and that they may have it more abundantly" (John 10:10). And He said in John 6:63, "It is the Spirit who gives life; the flesh profits nothing. The words that I speak to you are spirit, and they are life."

Jesus was saying the words He was speaking *then*

were the words that give life. The Law didn't give life. The gospel of grace gives life. Jesus also said to Peter, "You are already clean because of the word which I have spoken to you" (John 15:3). Jesus's words were the preaching of the new covenant of grace.

This demonic attempt to undermine the very words of Jesus should cause every Christian to reject these false teachers of grace, but unfortunately a spirit of deception is sweeping the church right now. Jesus's words are *all* true, and they are the *only* gospel.

The reason the very words of Jesus are under attack is that they clash with these teachers' wrong interpretations of grace. So in order to prove their false teaching, they must explain away why Jesus Himself preached against what they are saying.

Jesus said, "If anyone loves Me, he will keep My word; and My Father will love him, and We will come to him and make Our home with him. He who does not love Me does not keep My words; and the word which you hear is not Mine but the Father's who sent Me" (John 14:23–24). In this passage Jesus is saying that if we love Him we will obey His commands.

He later said, "These things I have spoken to you while being present with you. But the Helper, the Holy Spirit, whom the Father will send in My name, He will teach you all things, and bring to your remembrance *all things* that I said to you" (John 14:25–26, emphasis added). Jesus was saying that the Holy Spirit, who is the Spirit of grace, would bring to our remembrance *all* the things He said.

Why would the Holy Spirit remind us of all things if much of what Jesus said didn't apply to us because it was the Law and not part of the new covenant of grace? I could spend a whole book refuting this erroneous teaching, but suffice it to say that Jesus was preaching the good news of the gospel for all of us and was not preaching the Law.

What Is the Role of the Law in the Season of Grace?

I want to spend some time digging deep into the role of the Law in the face of grace. Hear me clearly when I tell you that much of what is being preached today about grace is simply not scriptural. It is a radical perversion of the truth that has not brought true freedom but has kept people in bondage and in sin.

I want you to clear your mind and honestly answer the following question: What thoughts and feelings come to you when hear somebody talk about the Law?

I have asked many people this question and the response is always something like this: "When I hear the word *law*, I think…legalism, religious, judgment, something bad or to be avoided, the Old Testament, bondage, pain." Rarely have I met a Christian who has a positive reaction when he hears the words *the law*. So let's begin here with our fundamental thoughts and feelings about the law of God and try to reconcile them with what God says about His law.

I warn you that this is going to be very eye-opening. Don't be afraid. What I am about to tell you will not put you in bondage. In the last chapter we dealt with the abuses and errors of legalism. In this section we are simply going to look at what God says about His law.

We read in Romans 7, "Therefore the law is holy, and the commandment holy and just and good....For we know that the law is spiritual, but I am carnal, sold under sin" (vv. 12, 14). It is important that you see what God's opinion of the Law is in the New Testament. He says the Law is *holy*, the Law is *just*, the Law is *good*, and the Law is *spiritual*.

That is a far cry from the list above that likens the Law to legalism, religious rules, judgment, something to be avoided, bondage, and pain. These feelings and beliefs about the Law are not based on Scripture. We have taken what God says is good and called it evil, and we have done this because we think the Law is what put us in bondage. The truth is, the Law was never the problem. The problem was and has always been *sin*. Let's look again at Romans 7.

> Therefore the law is holy, and the commandment holy and just and good. Has then what is good become death to me? Certainly not! *But sin, that it might appear sin, was producing death in me through what is good, so that sin through the commandment might become exceedingly sinful.* For we know that the law is spiritual, but I am carnal, sold under sin.
>
> —Romans 7:12–14,
> emphasis added

The Law didn't produce death. Sin produced the death. Jesus came not to do away with the Law but to fulfill it. He said, "Do not think that I came to destroy the Law or the Prophets. I did not come to destroy but to fulfill. For assuredly, I say to you, till heaven and earth pass away, one jot or one tittle will by no means pass from the law till all is fulfilled" (Matt. 5:17–18).

Jesus came to do away with the real problem, and that was sin. Let me make this very clear: sin is the problem. Sin is what produces death. The Law doesn't bring death; sin does. This is a very important distinction. Jesus came to deal with the root of our problem, which was sin. The Law exposed the sinfulness of sin. "But sin, that it might appear sin, was producing death in me through what is good, so that sin through the commandment might become exceedingly sinful" (Rom. 7:13).

God sent the holy Law to expose the real problem, which was our sin nature. The Law had only the power to expose our sin nature. It didn't have the power to deliver us from it. As a result, obedience to the Law could never produce righteousness because the Law could never deal with mankind's internal fallen nature. Jesus came to destroy the power of the sin nature and thus truly deliver us from bondage.

Romans 8:3 says, "For God has done what the Law could not do, [its power] being weakened by the flesh [the entire nature of man without the Holy Spirit]. Sending His own Son in the guise of sinful flesh and as an offering for sin, [God] condemned sin in the flesh [subdued, overcame, deprived it of its power over all who accept that sacrifice]" (AMP).

The Law is holy, just, good, and spiritual even today. It was, however, unable to deliver us from bondage because of sin. We need to stop calling something bad and religious that God calls good and holy. If God says in the New Testament that the Law is holy, then who are we to ever declare it anything else? We must come into agreement that the Law is good, just, holy, and spiritual.

If this is hard for you to swallow, that is proof that what you have been indoctrinated with for so long is a false teaching. If you don't believe the law of God is holy, just, good, and spiritual, then there is a lie deeply rooted within that you have believed to be the truth. All of God's words are holy. All of God's commandments are just and good. Everything God says in His Word is spiritual.

As I have declared over and over again, obedience to the Law will not win you favor with God. That is not because the Law isn't good and holy. It is because of sin. Apart from God, fallen man is incapable of total obedience to the Law. We see this truth declared in the Book of Romans:

> As it is written:
>
> *"There is none righteous, no, not one;*
> *There is none who understands;*
> *There is none who seeks after God.*
> *They have all turned aside;*
> *They have together become unprofitable;*
> *There is none who does good, no, not one."*
> *"Their throat is an open tomb;*
> *With their tongues they have practiced deceit";*
> *"The poison of asps is under their lips";*
> *"Whose mouth is full of cursing and bitterness."*
> *"Their feet are swift to shed blood;*
> *Destruction and misery are in their ways;*
> *And the way of peace they have not known."*
> *"There is no fear of God before their eyes."*

Now we know that whatever the law says, it says to those who are under the law, that every mouth may be stopped, and all the world may become guilty before God. *Therefore by the deeds of the law no flesh will be justified in His sight, for by the law is the knowledge of sin.* But now the righteousness of God apart from the law is revealed, being witnessed by the Law and the Prophets, even the righteousness of God, through faith in Jesus Christ, to all and on all who believe. For there is no difference; for all have sinned and fall short of the glory of God, being justified freely by His grace through the redemption that is in Christ Jesus, whom God set forth as a propitiation by His blood, through faith, to demonstrate His righteousness, because in His forbearance God had passed over the sins that were previously committed, to demonstrate at the present time His righteousness, that He might be just and the justifier of the one who has faith in Jesus.

—ROMANS 3:10–26,
emphasis added

So what then is the role of the Law in the Christian's life if we are not saved and justified by the Law? Does the Law have any place in the church? I would submit that the Law has a powerful place in the church. Let's see what the Epistles have to say about the role of the Law in our lives.

Every Scripture is God-breathed (given by His inspiration) and profitable for instruction, for reproof and conviction of sin, for correction of error and discipline in obedience, [and] for training in righteousness (in holy living, in conformity to

God's will in thought, purpose, and action), so that
the man of God may be complete and proficient,
well fitted and thoroughly equipped for every good
work.

—2 Timothy 3:16–17, amp

This passage says that every scripture is given by God.
That includes *all* of the Law. Put this in your spirit: we
are no longer required to obey the regulations of the
Law, but we are required to submit to the revelation of
the Law. Beneath the regulation of the Law is tremen-
dous revelation.

Jesus was constantly teaching His disciples the revelation that was under the regulation and telling them to
obey that revelation. Consider the following examples.

You have heard that it was said to those of old, "*You
shall not murder*, and whoever murders will be in
danger of the judgment." But I say to you that whoever is angry with his brother without a cause shall
be in danger of the judgment. And whoever says
to his brother, "Raca!" shall be in danger of the
council. But whoever says, "You fool!" shall be in
danger of hell fire.

—Matthew 5:21-22,
emphasis added

Jesus is saying, "You have heard that the Law says
don't murder, but I am going to give you the revelation
behind the Law: You must not hate. You must love even
your enemy."

You have heard that it was said to those of old,
"*You shall not commit adultery.*" But I say to you

that whoever looks at a woman to lust for her has
already committed adultery with her in his heart.

—MATTHEW 5:27-28,
emphasis added

Jesus is saying here, "The Law commands you not to
commit adultery, but the revelation behind the Law is
that adultery is a heart issue, so I am commanding you
not to lust."

> We are no longer required to obey the
> regulations of the Law, but we are required
> to submit to the revelation of the Law.

The Word of God—all of it—is good for training in
righteousness. It reveals to us God's nature and how we
are to live as children of God. It also exposes what sin is
so we can put off the old man and put on the new man.
The apostle Paul wrote:

But you have not so learned Christ, if indeed you
have heard Him and have been taught by Him, as
the truth is in Jesus: that you put off, concerning
your former conduct, the old man which grows
corrupt according to the deceitful lusts, and be
renewed in the spirit of your mind, and that you
put on the new man which was created according
to God, in true righteousness and holiness.

—EPHESIANS 4:20–24

The Law (and all of God's Word) in the life of the
believer is to reveal the holiness of God and show us how

we are to live. Again, you must look to the revelation, not the regulation. The regulation says do this or do that; the revelation always deals with the true heart motives.

> For the Word that God speaks is alive and full of power [making it active, operative, energizing, and effective]; it is sharper than any two-edged sword, penetrating to the dividing line of the breath of life (soul) and [the immortal] spirit, and of joints and marrow [of the deepest parts of our nature], exposing and sifting and analyzing and judging the very thoughts and purposes of the heart.
>
> —HEBREWS 4:12, AMP

I can't repeat this enough: you are never justified by the obeying the Law. You are justified by faith in Christ. However, we are required to pursue holiness and flee the fruitless deeds of darkness.

Does the Holy Spirit Convict Christians of Sin?

The false grace message teaches that the Holy Spirit never convicts believers of sin; He only convicts or convinces them that they are righteous because their sins past, present, and future were forgiven when Jesus died on the cross. These grace teachers claim that only the devil points out our sin.

The truth is, the closer we get to God, the more sensitive we become to His holiness and the more the Holy Spirit identifies areas in our lives that are sinful. Every revival in the history of the world has been marked by this one consistent truth: during a true move of God, even those who considered themselves godly came under deep conviction about their sinful states and repented. If you were to accept the false teaching that the Holy Spirit never convicts Christians of sin, you would have to throw out every recorded revival in history.

Now there is a world of difference between conviction and condemnation. Conviction is when the Holy Spirit identifies areas of disobedience in your life and moves on you to repent of them and yield that area to the lordship of Jesus Christ. Condemnation is that feeling of judgment and guilt that you can't seem to get free of. Second Corinthians 7:10 tells us, "For godly sorrow produces repentance leading to salvation, not to be regretted; but the sorrow of the world produces death."

When Paul wrote that verse, he was addressing a group of Christians. Godly sorrow, which came as a result of Paul's rebuke for their sin, produces a *sozo* salvation, a being made whole. This is not the born-again salvation, but the process of being made whole. The sorrow of the world is condemnation. Thanks be to God that "there is therefore now no condemnation to those who are in Christ Jesus, who do not walk according to the flesh, but according to the Spirit" (Rom. 8:1).

The Holy Spirit clearly convicts even believers of sin. The argument that the Holy Spirit doesn't convict Christians of sin comes from the verse that says, "And when He has come, He will convict the world of sin, and of righteousness, and of judgment: of sin, because they do not believe in Me; of righteousness, because I go to My Father and you see Me no more; of judgment, because the ruler of this world is judged" (John 16:8–11).

Those teaching the false grace message try to say that

the Holy Spirit will only convict the world of sin, not
Christians. This is intellectually dishonest, since the
passage in John 16 names three areas of conviction: sin,
righteousness, and judgment.

They also say that when Jesus says "you" in verse 10,
He is no longer referring to the believers He was talking
with previously but is referring to nonbelievers. Yet in
the context of verse 8 the passage refers to all of us. The
Greek word translated "world" in John 16:8 is the same
one used in John 3:16 when it says God so loved the
world that He gave His only begotten Son.

The word *you* in verse 10 is not in the original language. It was added to bring clarity. And those arguing
that the *you* refers only to believers must also explain
what exactly it means to be a believer. Was Judas a
believer? He was there with the disciples. These grace
teachers say that if you are born again, the Holy Spirit
will convict you only of your righteousness because
Jesus used "you" in John 16:10. But the people Jesus was
talking with in John 16 weren't born again yet because
Jesus hadn't died on the cross.

False grace teachers are trying to creatively interpret this passage to make a point that is not supported
in Scripture. The Holy Spirit convicts *all* of us. Thank
God He does, or I wouldn't know the difference between
right and wrong.

It is the Holy Spirit's job to convict us. The word *convict* is used in reference to Christians throughout the
New Testament. It comes from the Greek word *elegchō*
and means to expose, convict or reprimand, reprove,
rebuke, refute, show fault.[5] All of the following scriptures

use the word *elegchō* when speaking of the Holy Spirit's job to convict the body of Christ concerning sin:

> All Scripture *is* given by inspiration of God, and *is* profitable for doctrine, for *reproof* [conviction], for correction, for instruction in righteousness.
>
> —2 TIMOTHY 3:16,
> emphasis added

> Moreover if your brother sins against you, go and *tell* him *his fault* [convict] between you and him alone. If he hears you, you have gained your brother.
>
> —MATTHEW 18:15,
> emphasis added

> Do not receive an accusation against an elder except from two or three witnesses. Those who are sinning *rebuke* [convict] in the presence of all, that the rest also may fear.
>
> —1 TIMOTHY 5:19–20,
> emphasis added

> One of them, a prophet of their own, said, "Cretans are always liars, evil beasts, lazy gluttons." This testimony is true. Therefore *rebuke* [convict] them sharply, that they may be sound in the faith.
>
> —TITUS 1:12–13,
> emphasis added

> And you have forgotten the exhortation which speaks to you as to sons: "My son, do not despise the chastening of the LORD, nor be discouraged when you are *rebuked* [convicted] by Him."
>
> —HEBREWS 12:5,
> emphasis added

As many as I love, I *rebuke* [convict] and chasten.
Therefore be zealous and repent.

—Revelation 3:19,
emphasis added

Look at that last verse. Jesus Himself said in essence,
"If I love you, I will convict you." Convict you of what?
Sin, because He then says for us to be zealous and repent.
You don't repent of being convicted of being righteous.
You repent of sin.

Are Christians Required to Repent?

In Hebrews we are given the six foundational doctrines
of Christ. The very first one is repentance of dead works.
The word *repent* means to "change one's mind,"[6] but
more specifically, according to *Thayer's Greek Lexicon*
it means "to change one's mind for better, heartily to
amend with abhorrence of one's past sins."[7]

Charles Finney, who I believe was the greatest
American revivalist of all time, says of true repentance,
"If you have truly repented, you do not now love sin; you
do not now abstain from it through fear, and to avoid
punishment, but because you hate it."[8]

If you have not changed your thoughts and feelings
about sin, then you have not truly seen the Lord. Sin
is utterly detestable to the Christian who has had an
encounter with the holiness of God. If a person is simply
trying to get free from the guilt of sin and not pursuing
God to the point where he so abhors sin that he wants
to flee from it, then he has *not* truly had a revelation of
Christ.

The more you see God as He is, the more you will

be exposed and will want to turn from your sin. The problem in the church is that we preached a works-oriented lifestyle that never brought people to a real revelation of Christ. Or, as we see today, we preached a false grace message that is bent on relieving us from guilt and not changing our feelings about sin.

If you love sin, you hate God. First John 2:15–16 says, "Do not love the world or the things in the world. If anyone loves the world, the love of the Father is not in him. For all that is in the world—the lust of the flesh, the lust of the eyes, and the pride of life—is not of the Father but is of the world."

Repentance results from a brokenness that naturally comes as we receive increasing revelations of Christ. The following verses attest to this.

So I said:

"Woe is me, for I am undone!
Because I am a man of unclean lips,
And I dwell in the midst of a people of unclean
    lips;
For my eyes have seen the King,
The LORD of hosts."

—ISAIAH 6:5

For You do not desire sacrifice, or else I would
    give it;
You do not delight in burnt offering.
The sacrifices of God are a broken spirit,
A broken and a contrite heart—
These, O God, You will not despise.

—PSALM 51:16–17

For thus says the High and Lofty One
Who inhabits eternity, whose name is Holy:
"I dwell in the high and holy place,
With him who has a contrite and humble spirit,
To revive the spirit of the humble,
And to revive the heart of the contrite ones.
—ISAIAH 57:15

Brokenness is not something bad or something to be avoided. Brokenness, or godly sorrow, brings us to the place where we hate sin (2 Cor. 7:10). We see sin as something to be avoided not because it could lead to punishment but because it is opposed to God. We see sin as God does—utterly sinful. Seeing sin as God does isn't bad or wrong, but you would think it was by the way some of the false grace preachers teach about it.

Those who are truly pursuing God will continually experience seasons of godly sorrow, brokenness, and repentance that lead to an abhorrence of sin. The Holy Spirit will do this for us because God loves us. Why would God not convict us of the very things He hates and warn us to avoid them? Grace doesn't just free us from the guilt of sin; it also teaches and empowers us to stop sinning. Grace causes us to deny ungodliness and worldly lust. Grace empowers us to actually live a godly life in this world. Paul wrote:

For the grace of God that brings salvation has appeared to all men, teaching us that, denying ungodliness and worldly lusts, we should live soberly, righteously, and godly in the present age, looking for the blessed hope and glorious appearing of our great God and Savior Jesus Christ, who gave

Himself for us, that He might redeem us from every lawless deed and purify for Himself His own special people, zealous for good works. Speak these things, exhort, *and rebuke with all authority*. Let no one despise you.

—Titus 2:11–15,
emphasis added

Back in the sixties there was a philosophy that parents shouldn't correct their children. They should speak only positive things and never punish. This perverse idea failed miserably.

When I was a youth pastor in the late 1980s, there was a thirteen-year-old girl who started to attend our meetings. She was a mess; she would sneak out at night, getting high and getting drunk. After about three weeks she came up to me and told me about an incident that happened with her mother, who was a single parent. She said, "Last night I told my mother I was going to go out and get drunk again, and that I was gonna smoke pot, and I might have sex." She said, "Pastor Steve, my mom just let me go. She didn't even try and stop me. Pastor Steve, why doesn't my mom love me?"

This girl in all her rebellion wanted her mom to take a stand. She wanted her mom to warn and protect her, and stop her from getting involved in these sins. She saw, correctly, that her mom's failure to punish and correct her was a sign of a lack of love. Hebrews tells us that God corrects us because He loves us.

And have you [completely] forgotten the divine word of appeal and encouragement in which you are reasoned with and addressed as sons? My son, do not think lightly or scorn to submit to the correction and discipline of the Lord, nor lose courage and give up and faint when you are reproved or corrected by Him; for the Lord corrects and disciplines everyone whom He loves, and He punishes, even scourges, every son whom He accepts and welcomes to His heart and cherishes.

You must submit to and endure [correction] for discipline; God is dealing with you as with sons. For what son is there whom his father does not [thus] train and correct and discipline? Now if you are exempt from correction and left without discipline in which all [of God's children] share, then you are illegitimate offspring and not true sons [at all]. [*Prov. 3:11–12.*] Moreover, we have had earthly fathers who disciplined us and we yielded [to them] and respected [them for training us]. Shall we not much more cheerfully submit to the Father of spirits and so [truly] live?

For [our earthly fathers] disciplined us for only a short period of time and chastised us as seemed proper and good to them; but He disciplines us for our certain good, that we may become sharers in His own holiness. For the time being no discipline brings joy, but seems grievous and painful; but afterwards it yields a peaceable fruit of righteousness to those who have been trained by it [a harvest of fruit which consists in righteousness—in conformity to God's will in purpose, thought, and action, resulting in right living and right standing with God].

—Hebrews 12:5–11, amp

If you are not under conviction, if you are not disciplined unto repentance, if you are not trained in righteous living, then you are *not* a son of God! God loves you so much that He will convict, correct, and even punish you so you can learn to flee sin. This is not because God is mean or angry. He does this because of His great love for you. We see this throughout Scripture.

> Foolishness is bound up in the heart of a child; the rod of correction will drive it far from him.
> —PROVERBS 22:15

> Behold, happy is the man whom God corrects; therefore do not despise the chastening of the Almighty.
> —JOB 5:17

> As many as I love, I rebuke and chasten. Therefore be zealous and repent. Behold, I stand at the door and knock. If anyone hears My voice and opens the door, I will come in to him and dine with him, and he with Me.
> —REVELATION 3:19–20

> The rod and rebuke give wisdom, but a child left to himself brings shame to his mother.
> —PROVERBS 29:15

True grace has not come just to free us from judgment. It has come that we might have access to the power of God to live a life free from the bondage of sin.

Chapter 9

THE POWER OF HUMILITY

HUMILITY. WE HEAR it mentioned from time to time in church. We probably have all been accused of not being humble enough while all the time feeling sure that we are much more humble than people realize. If you ask ten people to describe the attributes of humility, you will probably get ten different answers. In this chapter I am going to make a feeble attempt to bring some clarity to this subject. Let's look at a passage in 1 Peter:

> Likewise you younger people, submit yourselves to your elders. Yes, all of you be submissive to one another, and be clothed with humility, for "God resists the proud, *but gives grace to the humble.*" Therefore humble yourselves under the mighty hand of God, that He may exalt you in due time, casting all your care upon Him, for He cares for you.
> —1 PETER 5:5–7,
> emphasis added

I believe one of the reasons we have so many different ideas about what humility is and is not is that most people judge humility based on their emotions. Does the action *feel* humble to them? Whether it's something they do or something they experience others doing, they use their emotions to judge whether the act was or was not humble.

It is amazing, but even most Christians rely on their emotions to reveal truth to them. The problem is that our emotions do not tell us the truth; they only reveal what we already believe. Our emotions are a reflection of something. They reflect what we already think.

In this chapter I am not going to deal with the emotions that are caused physiologically. Those result from hormonal and chemical reactions. Yet even in those cases our emotions are only reflecting something. They are not revealing truth. Our feelings don't reveal truth to us. Our feelings occur when a stimulus confronts what we already believe.

For instance, a person who wrongly believes a woman can't be a preacher often will have an initial negative emotional reaction when he or she sees a woman preacher. Of course, we Christians don't call it an emotional reaction; we call it being "grieved in our spirits." We say, "That grieved my spirit" or, "I had a check in my spirit." Often the reaction is not a spirit thing, but an emotional reaction based upon a preconceived way of thinking and believing.

I find this to be true especially in the area of "discerning" whether a person is humble or proud. As I have traveled abroad, I have noticed a very interesting phenomenon. I have found that in every region of the world people from one country are convinced that the people from a nearby country are proud and arrogant.

The French think the British are proud, and the British are convinced the French are proud. The Koreans think the Chinese are proud, the Chinese think the Japanese are proud, and so on. People in many countries think Americans are proud, and Americans are convinced others are the arrogant ones.

We have built into our cultures ideas of what pride and humility are, most of which aren't founded in the Scriptures. If we are going to get a breakthrough in this area, God is going to have to open our eyes so we can see what true humility looks like. Without this revelation, we will be stuck spiritually right where we are, because "God resists the proud, *but gives grace to the humble*" (James 4:6, emphasis added).

There is a place called grace where everything we need is. We have already discovered how grace is multiplied through the revelation knowledge of God. We have discovered the means God uses to bring that revelation knowledge to us. However, as we saw in chapter 2 through the parable of the seed and the sower, we need humility to pass from one stage of revelation to the next.

Each stage requires a greater degree of humility. One degree of humility is required to actually accept the Word. Then another degree of humility is required to pass through the test of failures. When the Word starts to prosper in our lives, another degree of humility is required to keep from getting sidetracked by the pleasures of this world or the deceitfulness of success. Finally, the greatest degree of humility is required to produce fruit thirty, sixty, and a hundredfold.

There is a place called grace where everything we need is. Humility is the doorway to that place. This is why we must grab hold of this revelation if we are going to progress any further.

The Cloak of Humility

Through the years I have read many books by Christian authors, many of which have greatly blessed me. But of all these books, one stands out more than the rest.

I was preaching down in Florida back in 1997. The church was hungry for God, and I was scheduled to be there for a whole week. I was staying with the pastor, and on that Monday around noon the Spirit of God fell upon me in a very unusual way in my room at the pastor's house. The presence of God was so thick it was almost more than I could bear. All I could do was pray and worship God.

The pastor had been out that morning but returned home after an hour or so. When he walked into the house, he too was struck by the power of God's presence. We proceeded to just stay on our knees and pray for a couple of hours. While praying, God spoke to me and said, "Son, this church is going to have an incredible breakthrough this week, and you are going to have one too."

The service that night was awesome. The next day I went to the Christian bookstore the pastor operated. I was going to buy a book just to be supportive of the business venture. While looking over the books, one seemed to grab my attention. I had heard of the book but didn't know much about it.

So I bought a copy of the book *The Final Quest* by Rick Joyner. I left the store and went back to the pastor's home to start reading. In this book Rick describes an incredible vision he had about a great and final battle between light and darkness. I read the book from cover to cover the first day, and the whole time I was overwhelmed by a sense of God's presence.

As I lay in bed that night after the church service, the Spirit of God fell on me. I began to cry tears of repentance. A brokenness came upon me. I wept for hours and then started to read the book again more slowly. This time it took me eight days to finish it.

As I read the book, I felt waves of the Holy Spirit's presence come upon me, and I would start to weep again. This second time I read the book, something changed. I was no longer reading a book; I was experiencing it. It was as if I had received the vision myself. I saw everything Rick described!

These eight days changed my life forever. Of all the things Rick described in the vision, one that struck me profoundly was the cloak of humility. I realized that without this cloak we would all be blinded by pride. In the vision those who had greater encounters with God needed the cloak of humility the most. I left that experience longing for this elusive characteristic of Christ called humility.

I have to be honest; until that time in my life I knew I needed humility but never really desired it. After that encounter I longed for true humility in my life and realized I didn't have a clue what it really was.

Grace to the Humble

James 4:6 says, "But He gives more grace. Therefore He says: 'God resists the proud, but gives grace to the humble.'" This elusive attribute called humility is the doorway to a place called grace. I have cried out to God many times, asking Him, "What is humility?" I didn't want some pat religious answer.

Some people think humility is expressed through weakness. This is a popular notion and is usually based on Paul's writings in 2 Corinthians:

> And He said to me, "My grace is sufficient for you, for *My strength is made perfect in weakness*." Therefore most gladly *I will rather boast in my infirmities*, that the power of Christ may rest upon me. Therefore I take pleasure in infirmities, in reproaches, in needs, in persecutions, in distresses, for Christ's sake. *For when I am weak, then I am strong.*
>
> —2 Corinthians 12:9–10,
> emphasis added

Now, based on what we have already learned—that grace is the favor of God that gives us access to the power of God for everything we need for life and godliness— this verse would seem to confirm that humility, which is the doorway to grace, is expressed in weakness. This is very true on one hand but very wrong on another.

The problem comes from not understanding the end result. Some view weak people as humble and strong people as proud. However, the truly humble person fully recognizes his own weaknesses and has learned to rely upon the grace (or favor) of God to gain access to the power of God so he can be strong.

Look again at what Paul says: "For when I am weak, *then I am strong.*" He didn't say he stayed weak. When he walked in true humility, when he learned to not rely upon his own abilities and to lean on the favor of God and then access the power of God, Paul won the victory. He became strong.

Let's look at this a little further. Paul's complaint in 2 Corinthians 12 was about the thorn in his flesh, the tormenting demons he was facing.

> And lest I should be exalted above measure by the abundance of the revelations, a *thorn in the flesh* was given to me, *a messenger of Satan to buffet me*, lest I be exalted above measure.
>
> —2 Corinthians 12:7, emphasis added

Over the years there has been much debate about what this thorn was. I believe the message is plain. Paul clearly says it was "a messenger of Satan." That means this was spiritual warfare. Paul was battling demon powers. The Bible says He cried out to God: "Concerning this thing *I pleaded with the Lord three times* that it might depart from me" (2 Cor. 12:8, emphasis added).

> The truly humble person fully recognizes his own weaknesses and has learned to rely upon the grace (or favor) of God to gain access to the power of God so he can be strong.

God responded: *"My grace is sufficient for you,* for My strength is made perfect in weakness" (2 Cor. 12:9, emphasis added). Many have wrongly interpreted this response as God saying, "Just put up with it, Paul. I am not going to deliver you. It is My will for you to have this torment."

Although I understand how people can interpret this scripture this way, I believe it is a total misunderstanding of what God was really saying. The misconception comes because people don't know what grace is. Let's place the definition for grace that we have received in this book into this verse and see if it makes a difference in our understanding.

God says, *"My grace*—the underserved, unmerited favor that has given you access to My power for everything you need for life and godliness—*is sufficient.* Paul, when you are weak and feeble, My favor will give you access to all the power you need to be strong. In this, Paul, I will be glorified."

Now look again at what 2 Corinthians 12:9 says, "Therefore most gladly *I will rather boast in my infirmities, that the power of Christ may rest upon me*" (emphasis added). Paul is saying, "I will boast in my weakness that the power of Christ may rest on me. If I humble myself by not relying upon my strength but upon God's strength, then I have access by grace to the power of Christ."

If the power of Christ is resting upon Paul, is he still weak? How could he be? Second Corinthians 12:9 says the *dunamis* of Christ—the miracle-working *power* of God—is resting upon him. So this is what was happening in this exchange in 2 Corinthians 12: Paul, not understanding the power he had access to, asked God to remove the tormenting demons. God said, "No, you do it." In other words, He basically said, "Paul, I have given you favor that has given you access to My power to overcome this tormenting spirit. You pick up the weapons of your warfare and fight."

This is where Paul learned spiritual warfare and then was able to teach his revelation to all of us. He wrote:

> For the weapons of our warfare are not carnal but mighty in God for pulling down strongholds.
> —2 CORINTHIANS 10:4

And:

> For *we do not wrestle against flesh and blood*, but against principalities, against powers, against the rulers of the darkness of this age, against spiritual hosts of wickedness in the heavenly places. Therefore take up the whole armor of God, *that you may be able to withstand in the evil day*, and having done all, to stand.
> —EPHESIANS 6:12–13,
> emphasis added

Jesus told His disciples: "'Assuredly, I say to you, whatever you bind on earth will be bound in heaven, and whatever you loose on earth will be loosed in heaven'" (Matt. 18:18). The same is true for us. Then in the Gospel of Luke, Jesus said, "Behold, *I give you the authority* to trample on serpents and scorpions, and over all the power of the enemy, *and nothing shall by any means hurt you*" (Luke 10:19, emphasis added).

In 2 Corinthians 12 God wasn't telling Paul to walk around in weakness. He was telling Paul that through humility—the recognition that he has nothing without God—He would give him access to all the power he would need to deal with the warfare he was facing. Weakness is not a sign of humility.

Poor and Humble

"Brother Steve, it is my job to keep the pastor poor and humble." An elder of a church actually said that to me one time. He truly believed that by keeping the pastor poor, he would keep him humble. Poverty does *not* produce one ounce of humility.

If God "gives grace to the humble" (James 4:6), and grace gives us access to the power of God, then those who are poor would have the greatest power of God at work in their lives. The inner cities would be booming with revival. Unfortunately this is often not the case. Where you find poverty, you find higher rates of crime, violence, drug use, vices, and all forms of debauchery.

I am not saying that the middle class and wealthy neighborhoods don't have these problems. I am only saying that if grace was being released because of humility that was produced by poverty, then you would think these poor places would have fewer sins, not more. Poverty does not produce humility, and people living in poverty do not bring God glory.

Poverty Looks Nothing Like Heaven

Just as there is nothing spiritual about being poor, there isn't anything spiritual about being rich. Neither wealth nor poverty produces spirituality. Neither wealth nor poverty can accurately tell us about a person's relationship with God.

Although I am addressing the lie that poverty makes

people humble and wealth makes people proud, I know there also are those who teach that if you're in a right relationship with God, you'll be wealthy. This too is misleading. In this book we have been learning how to tap into the favor of God for everything we need for life, but that doesn't mean God is a spiritual ATM machine.

It is arrogant for anyone to think they can use some spiritual formula to force the hand of God to give them whatever they want. That thinking is a stench in the nostrils of God. Truly accessing the favor of God requires humility. It requires a denial of self. This is why many preach about the favor of God but so few truly exemplify it. They think the favor of God is measured in material things and fame. They are dead wrong, and we will deal with that later in this book.

For the sake of this chapter, though, I want to expose the lie that poverty somehow produces humility. God is not poor. He lacks nothing, and we are His children. Second Corinthians 8:9 says, "For you know the grace of our Lord Jesus Christ, that though He was rich, yet for your sakes He became poor, that you through His poverty might become rich."

Weakness doesn't produce humility and neither does poverty. Humility doesn't mean you're shy, quiet, softspoken, self-deprecating, or anything similar. Humility is a condition of the heart. True humility is expressed through a deep belief that you're nothing without God and that without Jesus's sacrifice you deserve to spend an eternity in hell. These are not just nice words; humility requires a true heart revelation. You must decrease, and He must increase.

Consider these words from some truly humble mighty men of God:

John the Baptist

> He must increase, but *I must decrease.* He who comes from above is above all; he who is of the earth is earthly and speaks of the earth. *He who comes from heaven is above all.*
>
> —JOHN 3:30–31,
> emphasis added

Paul

> *I have been crucified* with Christ; *it is no longer I who live,* but Christ lives in me; and the life which I now live in the flesh I live by faith in the Son of God, who loved me and gave Himself for me.
>
> —GALATIANS 2:20,
> emphasis added

> And those who are Christ's have crucified the flesh with its passions and desires.
>
> —GALATIANS 5:24,
> emphasis added

> But God forbid that I should boast except in the cross of our Lord Jesus Christ, by whom *the world has been crucified to me, and I to the world.*
>
> —GALATIANS 6:14,
> emphasis added

> *But what things were gain to me, these I have counted loss for Christ.* Yet indeed *I also count all things loss for the excellence of the knowledge of*

> *Christ Jesus* my Lord, for whom I have suffered *the loss of all things*, and count them as rubbish, *that I may gain Christ...that I may know Him* and the power of His resurrection, and the fellowship of His sufferings, *being conformed to His death.*
> —PHILIPPIANS 3:7–8, 10,
> emphasis added

Peter

> Therefore, since Christ suffered for us in the flesh, arm yourselves also with the same mind, for he who has suffered in the flesh has ceased from sin, *that he no longer should live the rest of his time in the flesh for the lusts of men, but for the will of God.*
> —1 PETER 4:1–2,
> emphasis added

Jesus also exposed to us the true nature of humility throughout His life. One of the best descriptions of humility is found in Philippians, and it is referring to Christ:

> *Let this mind be in you which was also in Christ Jesus,* who, being in the form of God, did not consider it robbery to be equal with God, *but made Himself of no reputation, taking the form of a bondservant,* and coming in the likeness of men. And being found in appearance as a man, *He humbled Himself and became obedient to the point of death,* even the death of the cross.
> —PHILIPPIANS 2:5–8,
> emphasis added

There are several points in the passage above that I want us to look at quickly. There are other important truths in these verses, but I believe the following points are key in helping us to walk in humility as Jesus did.

1. Letting His mind be in us

First, we are commanded to have the same mind as Christ. The Amplified Bible translates Philippians 2:5 to say we are to let Christ be our example. We are to take on the same attitude that He had toward our lives here on earth.

Jesus and only Jesus is our example. That is why it is so crazy for people to compare themselves with others to determine their humility. "Well, I'm more humble than so-and-so," they think to themselves. The only true standard is Christ. Everything else is pride. Jesus is our living example of humility. We must take on *His* mind-set.

2. Making ourselves of no reputation

Jesus was fully God, yet He was willing to leave the glory He had in heaven and all His divine attributes to come here in the form of a man. Talk about denying oneself! Some people are barely willing to give up their favorite seat in the church.

We demand to be honored, to have our praises sung and our names recognized. Some say, "Don't disrespect me." I have seen so many Christians, even pastors, get mad in church because they feel somebody didn't honor them appropriately.

Some preachers demand the finest hotels, fanciest cars, and personal butlers all because they feel they deserve it. I know of ministers who have their drivers buckle them in because apparently fastening their own seat belts is beneath them. From the pulpit to the pew, the stench of pride rises up before the throne of God.

Many times behind the scenes at major Christian events, I have seen preachers posture themselves to get the most visible seats on the platform. They demand to be publicly honored or they won't attend. Others demand that their names be printed at the top of the event advertisements. They fight to be *the* guy or gal at the meeting. It is self-promotion and self-exaltation, plain and simple.

These preachers wrongly believe they are under the favor of God because of the ministry gifts that flow through their lives. If God can anoint a donkey to speak, it is not praise from heaven when God anoints a man. Praise from heaven is *never* measured in a man's gifting.

Jesus had the ultimate right to demand honor and respect. He had the ultimate right to hold on to His position and glory. Jesus came and set an example for us. The way up to the throne is down.

Jesus was willing to associate with those who were rejected by the religious community. He was willing to be scorned, mocked, spit upon, defamed, lied about, and ultimately betrayed without even lifting a voice in protest.

This is not what we see today in much of the church. I have attended events at which the main conference speakers would get offended if the other ministers didn't spend five or ten minutes singing their praises. I even had a minister rebuke me publicly because when I preached at his conference I didn't take time out of the thirty minutes I had been given to sing his praises.

It wasn't that I didn't honor him. I had only thirty minutes to share the word God had given me to change these people's lives. Wasting some of that time to stroke the ego of this famous minister wasn't even on my radar screen.

The Scriptures do say that we are to give honor to whom honor is due (Rom. 13:7). We are to give honor but never require it for ourselves.

The *lust* for *fame* is so ingrained into our American and Western culture that we hardly even recognize it anymore. We have deluded ourselves into thinking that seeking attention and fame is the will of God and a sign of His favor. Yet the Scriptures scream to us another standard:

> He must increase, but I must decrease.
>
> —JOHN 3:30

> Most assuredly, I say to you, *unless a grain of wheat falls into the ground and dies, it remains alone*; but if it dies, it produces much grain. *He who loves his life will lose it*, and he who hates his life in this world will keep it for eternal life.
>
> —JOHN 12:24–25,
> emphasis added

There are many ministers who claim to have died to self, yet this very declaration seems to fly in the face of the facts. It seems to me that a person who has truly died to self would probably not spend much time declaring it to others. The one who is truly dead to himself desires only to draw attention to Christ.

Paul's life, as he matured in Christ, reflected a

self-loathing and self-devaluing, not self-exaltation. He wrote in 1 Timothy 1:15, "This is a faithful saying and worthy of all acceptance, that Christ Jesus came into the world to save sinners, *of whom I am chief*" (emphasis added).

> We are to give honor but never
> require it for ourselves.

As I write this, I am also so very aware that I have not arrived at this place of death to myself and my reputation. There is a war raging for our hearts. The battle is internal and works upon our base desires for self-actualization and self-esteem.

We live in a success-driven culture that tells us that we need to feed our flesh to gain a sense of personal value and worth. We long to be "somebody" in the eyes of the world or of Christendom. So many of us struggle with a deep sense of inferiority when we don't measure up to the elusive standards of success that are based on how much money, popularity, influence, or spiritual gifting we have. These are not even to be on our radar screens in the way we measure our worth, yet they consume us and drive our choices.

Within the body of Christ, people flock from one ministry to another desiring to be connected with something they perceive to be successful. If they can't attain some level of fame and power themselves, they will attach to those who are excelling so they can, in a de facto way, ride the wave of another's "success."

That is why we see ministers soar to the heights of popularity only to quickly fade into obscurity. The body flocked to them when they were perceived to be the "in thing," but those same Christians left for the next superstar who came on the scene.

If a church is going through a struggle, often large groups of members will leave. They claim to have been called to that church, but when times get rough, they are suddenly called to the new "in" ministry down the street. Let's face it—we all love to be on the winning team. We love to feel like we are part of something that is "happening." We love to feel like we have an edge over others, like we've found a special measure of the favor of God.

This is also why, when a brother or sister falls, many in Christendom discard them. It is why we kill our wounded. We kill them not because of whatever sin they committed but because of how their failure makes us look. Their sin reflects upon our reputation, therefore we will distance ourselves from them and often attack them at their weakest points so we can protect our precious reputations.

It is difficult for us to find modern examples of people who model the humility of Christ. It is not because they don't exist—they do. But because they are so dead to their own reputations, they often go unnoticed. Throughout the Scriptures and history many of God's most humble servants were not honored and recognized in their day. If we truly want the grace and favor of God, then we are going to have to make ourselves of *no* reputation.

3. Taking the form of a bondservant

There has been a surge of teaching in recent decades about becoming a servant. Ministers taught people about being armor bearers and serving their pastors. While being a servant is scriptural, some of this teaching has become skewed. It is only a partial and often self-serving teaching on servanthood.

I call this trend the "serve until" movement. The basic teaching goes this way: If you want to be used by God, serve the man or woman of God. If you want their anointing, serve them. If you want their favor and success, you must serve them. The unspoken part of this is "until"—*until* you build your own ministry; *until* you become successful; *until* you have fame, money, and popularity. Then you can teach others the same and become the one who is served.

This is the pattern that has arisen. We teach others to serve us. We use genuine biblical principles to support this teaching, yet we arrive at a place where we are the served and no longer the servants. The truth is, the more we mature, the more we are to become servants of all.

> Jesus came to serve. He didn't come for His own comfort and pleasure. He came to fulfill the will of the Father.

I remember the several times I had the privilege to work beside Dr. Edwin Louis Cole, founder of the Christian Men's Network and author of the best seller *Maximized Manhood*. I was so impressed by his deep and true humility. He always showed such a servant's heart. He was never too high and mighty for anybody.

I went to his hotel room one time to escort him to the service where he was to preach. He didn't really want an escort, but he didn't know exactly where the service was being held. As he came out the door, I offered to carry his books for him, but he said he didn't need me to do that. He was more interested in talking with me, asking me who I was and about my life.

At this point in my ministry I had worked with many prominent preachers. Most of them required people to behave as though they were in the presence of a king. If they didn't think you were "somebody," they would often ignore the fact that you were even there. Dr. Cole was different. He was genuinely interested in everybody, no matter what their station in life. He had a way of touching you with his authenticity and Christlike humility.

He never wanted fanfare. He never wanted praise from men. All he wanted was to bring each person the life-changing truths that God had shown him. He wanted to serve.

Jesus came to serve. He didn't come for His own comfort and pleasure. He came to fulfill the will of the Father.

We all need to be servants, not just servants until we can be served. The most consistent quality of mature saints, especially leaders in the body of Christ, should be that they are servants. The apostle Paul said, "For though I am free from all men, *I have made myself a servant to all*, that I might win the more" (1 Cor. 9:19, emphasis added).

We also see this modeled in the life of Jesus:

Then Jesus spoke to the multitudes and to His disciples, saying: "The scribes and the Pharisees sit in Moses' seat. Therefore whatever they tell you to observe, that observe and do, *but do not do according to their works; for they say, and do not do.* For they bind heavy burdens, hard to bear, and lay them on men's shoulders; but they themselves will not move them with one of their fingers. *But all their works they do to be seen by men.* They make their phylacteries broad and enlarge the borders of their garments. *They love the best places at feasts, the best seats in the synagogues, greetings in the marketplaces, and to be called by men, 'Rabbi, Rabbi.'* But you, do not be called *'Rabbi'; for One is your Teacher, the Christ, and you are all brethren.* Do not call anyone on earth your father; for One is your Father, He who is in heaven. And do not be called teachers; for One is your Teacher, the Christ. *But he who is greatest among you shall be your servant. And whoever exalts himself will be humbled, and he who humbles himself will be exalted.*

"But woe to you, scribes and Pharisees, hypocrites! For you shut up the kingdom of heaven against men; for you neither go in yourselves, nor do you allow those who are entering to go in. Woe to you, scribes and Pharisees, hypocrites! For you devour widows' houses, and for a pretense make long prayers. Therefore you will receive greater condemnation.

"Woe to you, scribes and Pharisees, hypocrites! *For you travel land and sea to win one proselyte,*

*and when he is won, you make him twice as much
a son of hell as yourselves."*
—MATTHEW 23:1–15,
emphasis added

It's not hard to see some of today's highly visible Christian ministries falling into the same categories as the Pharisees.

- The leaders of Jesus's day demanded much from the people, but they wouldn't do the same things themselves. Today we teach others to serve the minister, but the minister won't serve.

- The Pharisees loved to be honored and expected the best seats. We've already discussed this at length. This is definitely happening today.

- The religious leaders demanded to be addressed by their titles. Today everybody wants to be called bishop, apostle, prophet, etc. There is nothing wrong with honoring our leaders. But it is wrong when the leader demands that a certain title be used primarily because it makes him feel superior. Oftentimes these titles are more about self-exaltation than the advancement of the kingdom.

We as leaders are *not* to lord over people. We are to minister to them as servants of Christ. Consider these qualities of a good servant:

- A good servant takes care of others before himself.

- A good servant works for the exaltation of others, not himself.

- A good servant expects *no* recognition for his service since it is his duty to serve.

- A good servant is faithful with what belongs to another.

- A good servant does all things for the honor of the one he serves.

Jesus said:

> And which of you, having a servant plowing or tending sheep, will say to him when he has come in from the field, "Come at once and sit down to eat"? But will he not rather say to him, "Prepare something for my supper, and gird yourself and serve me till I have eaten and drunk, and afterward you will eat and drink"? Does he thank that servant because he did the things that were commanded him? I think not. So likewise you, *when you have done all those things which you are commanded, say, "We are unprofitable servants. We have done what was our duty to do."*
>
> —Luke 17:7–10,
> emphasis added

Can you imagine what the church would be like if we all had this attitude, not only toward Jesus but also toward one another? Humility is the key to receiving the grace of God. God gives grace to the humble.

Grace is the favor of God that gives us access to the power of God for everything we need for life and godliness. Humility is the doorway to that favor.

True humility is the doorway to the presence of God from which all things flow.

It all really makes sense if you think about it. Grace is multiplied through the knowledge of God. We cannot receive the knowledge of God through our own understanding. It comes from God. God resists the proud. The Holy Spirit withdraws from the proud. As long as we are full of pride, we will not understand the mysteries of God:

> But the natural man does not receive the things of the Spirit of God, for they are foolishness to him; nor can he know them, because they are spiritually discerned.
> —1 CORINTHIANS 2:14

> He answered and said to them, "Because it has been given to you to know the mysteries of the kingdom of heaven, but to them it has not been given. For whoever has, to him more will be given, and he will have abundance; but whoever does not have, even what he has will be taken away from him. Therefore I speak to them in parables, because seeing they do not see, and hearing they do not hear, nor do they understand."
> —MATTHEW 13:11–13

> However, when He, the Spirit of truth, has come,
> He will guide you into all truth; for He will not
> speak on His own authority, but whatever He hears
> He will speak; and He will tell you things to come.
> He will glorify Me, for He will take of what is Mine
> and declare it to you.
>
> —JOHN 16:13–14

True humility is the doorway to the presence of God from which all things flow. It is expressed in the decreasing of ourselves and the exaltation of Christ and His Word above everything in our lives. It is manifested in our embracing the cross and dying to ourselves. We are to take on the very example of Christ.

May we all long for the same mind that was in Christ to also be in us. May God deliver us from the megalomania that for too long has been so prevalent in the church.

Chapter 10

A PLACE CALLED GRACE

THERE IS A place called grace where everything you need is. We have traveled down an awesome path of revelation so far. All of this has been to lead us to the place called grace. This place is where all the parts of this revelation come together. This is the place God has been trying to bring us back to ever since the fall of man.

Jesus came to restore us to this place. His blood, shed on the cross, gives us access to this place. And it is in this place that everything in our lives will change.

The Scriptures refer to this place in the Book of Hebrews.

> Seeing then that we have a great High Priest who has passed through the heavens, Jesus the Son of God, let us hold fast our confession. For we do not have a High Priest who cannot sympathize with our weaknesses, but was in all points tempted as we are, yet without sin. *Let us therefore come boldly to the throne of grace, that we may obtain mercy and find grace to help in time of need.*
> —HEBREWS 4:14–16,
> emphasis added

The "throne of grace" mentioned in the passage above is the throne of God. The writer of Hebrews is saying for us to come boldly to the throne of grace that we may obtain mercy for all our sins and failures and that we may obtain grace (favor) to help us in our time of *need*.

Everything we have looked at in this book is summed up in this one verse. The throne of grace, the throne of God's presence, is the place where we find everything we need.

In the last several years there has been much emphasis in Christian circles on worship and abiding in the presence of God. Many anointed authors have written incredible books about the throne room presence of God. Prophetic ministers have been speaking about a coming increase in the revelation of God's presence.

> The throne of grace, the throne of God's presence, is the place where we find everything we need.

With all of the great teaching out there, I am not going to repeat what has already been said. I am, however, going to touch on a few key points of revelation in regard to approaching the throne.

What Is the Throne of Grace?

This subject of the throne room presence of God is very near and dear to my heart. If anyone talks with me about God for long, it seems the conversation always ends up at His throne room.

When I talk about entering the throne room presence of God, I am not simply speaking about that feeling you get when you are in a good worship service. The reality is that you can feel God's presence and never even come close to entering His throne room. Many people feel the presence of God. Even the unsaved and the backslidden can feel the presence of God, but that doesn't mean that they have entered into the throne room.

The throne of God is also known as the secret place. Psalm 91:1 says, "He who dwells in *the secret place of the Most High* shall abide under the shadow of the Almighty" (emphasis added). There is a reason it is called the secret place. It's because this place is hidden. Not everyone can access this place in God's presence. Some people may think that's not fair, but it actually is consistent with Scripture. Not everyone can access the throne, but that doesn't mean they can't access it one day. It is because of their present state that they cannot enter.

This secret place is endless in depth, boundless in glory, and indescribable in power. Most Western Christians have never gone there, including many who think they have. We have set the watermark so low that most don't even aspire to encounter the presence of God in a deeper way.

Too many Christians are easily satisfied with just a slight sensation of the presence of God, with warm, peaceful feelings and a sense of comfort. However, the secret place is not a place of warm fuzzies. It is a place where we encounter God in His fullness. It is a place where we will tremble at His presence. It is a place where the deepest and darkest secrets of our hearts will be exposed. It is a place where the light of the knowledge of the glory of God will strip us bare before His holiness.

The Scriptures tell us that when the prophet Isaiah encountered the throne of God, he was undone.

> In the year that King Uzziah died, *I saw the Lord sitting on a throne*, high and lifted up, and the train of His robe filled the temple. Above it stood seraphim; each one had six wings: with two he covered his face, with two he covered his feet, and with two he flew. And one cried to another and said: "Holy, holy, holy is the LORD of hosts; the whole earth is full of His glory!" And the posts of the door were shaken by the voice of him who cried out, and the house was filled with smoke. *So I said: "Woe is me, for I am undone! Because I am a man of unclean lips, and I dwell in the midst of a people of unclean lips; for my eyes have seen the King, the Lord of hosts."*
>
> —ISAIAH 6:1–5,
> emphasis added

I don't know about you, but this hasn't been my experience in a typical Sunday morning service or even at most prayer meetings. Being in God's presence caused Isaiah to cry out. This God-fearing, righteous-living, totally consecrated man became filled with the awareness of his own wickedness when he entered the throne room of God.

He couldn't do anything but confess his own sins and the sins of his people. I have been in only a few meetings where this kind of encounter has taken place. When it did, I didn't experience warm fuzzies. God's presence was terrifying. I was struck with the fear of the Lord.

Although we are not to be afraid of God, the Bible tells us we are to fear Him, because He is worthy of honor and reverence.

> *Tremble*, O earth, *at the presence of the Lord*, at the presence of the God of Jacob.
>
> —Psalm 114:7,
> emphasis added

> *Clouds and darkness surround Him*; righteousness and justice are the foundation of His throne. *A fire goes before Him*, and burns up His enemies round about. His lightnings light the world; the earth sees and trembles. *The mountains melt like wax at the presence of the Lord, at the presence of the Lord of the whole earth.*
>
> —Psalm 97:2–5,
> emphasis added

A deep comfort is found in the secret place, but that peace comes only after the fear of the Lord.

> Then one of the seraphim flew to me, having in his hand a live coal which he had taken with the tongs from the altar. And he touched my mouth with it, and said: "Behold, this has touched your lips; your iniquity is taken away, and your sin purged."
>
> —Isaiah 6:6–7,
> emphasis added

> *Repent* therefore and be converted, that your sins
> may be blotted out, so that *times of refreshing may
> come from the presence of the Lord.*
>
> —Acts 3:19,
> emphasis added

Where did we ever get the idea that the presence of God was something we could casually enter into and out of? How deceived we have become when we think we can enter His throne room presence while we walk in blatant sin. How dare we treat His presence as common!

We show up to services unrepentant, unconvicted, and unmoved. We crawl in late and want to leave early. We complain when the worship lasts too long or the preacher doesn't let us out "on time." We sing our few choruses, clap our hands, and say hallelujah. All the while our minds are only half there. We've spent most of that time thinking about our problems, our needs; what so-and-so is doing or wearing; that the music is too loud, soft, good, or not good.

If we were honest, most of us would have to admit that during the worship time at most church services, our minds are only partially focused on God, if at all. Many churchgoers are simply spectators. They are watching the worship leaders press in to God and enjoying the performance. In some parts of the world the churches even call it performance worship, as if to say, "Come and watch me get intimate with God."

When we truly enter into the throne room of God, His presence will be the only thing on our minds. We will be overwhelmed with His glory. In this place often you'll lose all sense of time and place. You may not even be sure whether you're still in this world or have transcended to the third heaven.

The throne room of God is unmistakable. When you have entered it, you'll know. There are many around the world who understand what I am talking about. Most, however, are in nations that persecute Christians. Those believers can't play church because simply going to a worship service could cost them their lives.

> When we truly enter into the throne room of God, His presence will be the only thing on our minds.

Yet here in the West, if we feel a little touch of His presence, a tear may well up in our eyes, and we'll walk out and say it was a glorious service. How far short we have fallen when we settled for so much less than God's best! The good news is that God has made a way for us to enter this glorious and terrifying place of His presence. If we will simply follow His path, we will reach this place called grace, where everything we need is.

Chapter 11

ENTERING THE
SECRET PLACE

GOD REVEALS TO us many truths through the tabernacle of the Old Testament. In particular He spends a significant amount of time revealing to us truths about His throne room presence and how we can enter into it.

As I said before, not everyone can enter into the throne room presence of God. When God's presence dwelled in the tabernacle, there were places everybody could enter, such as the outer court, and there were places only God's people could enter, such as the inner court. There were places only the priests could enter and even one room that only the high priest could enter, and even at that he could enter only once a year. This was the most restricted place because it was also the place with the greatest manifestation of God's presence—the holy of holies.

The writer of Hebrews tells us to come boldly to the throne of grace that we may obtain mercy and find grace to help in time of need. It is important to realize that there is a protocol to entering God's throne room. We will look at that protocol at length later in this book.

Right now I want to clarify something that is often misunderstood about the anointing and the throne room presence of God. Most people think they are one and the same. This is simply not true. The anointing is the authorization of God to fulfill a specific ministry. You can be anointed and be denied access to the throne room presence of God, as we see in this passage from Ezekiel.

> "And the Levites who went far from Me, when Israel went astray, who strayed away from Me after their idols, they shall bear their iniquity. Yet they shall be ministers in My sanctuary, as gatekeepers of the house and ministers of the house; they shall slay the burnt offering and the sacrifice for the people, and they shall stand before them to minister to them. Because they ministered to them before their idols and caused the house of Israel to fall into iniquity, therefore I have raised My hand in an oath against them," says the Lord GOD, "that they shall bear their iniquity. And they shall not come near Me to minister to Me as priest, nor come near any of My holy things, nor into the Most Holy Place; but they shall bear their shame and their abominations which they have committed. Nevertheless I will make them keep charge of the temple, for all its work, and for all that has to be done in it.
>
> "But the priests, the Levites, the sons of Zadok, who kept charge of My sanctuary when the children of Israel went astray from Me, they shall come near Me to minister to Me; and they shall stand before Me to offer to Me the fat and the blood," says the Lord GOD. "They shall enter My sanctuary,

and they shall come near My table to minister to
Me, and they shall keep My charge."
—Ezekiel 44:10–16

This passage of Scripture is powerful. God said the
Levites, who had backslidden and led the people to worship idols, still had a place in ministry. Yet even though
they had repented, their ministry was limited. This was
their punishment: they were allowed to minister to the
people but were forbidden to come before the presence
of God.

Today we place great value on the anointing and
public ministry. God, however, places value on the time
we spend ministering to Him. God allows the ones who
are faithful to seek Him above all else to come before
His presence.

The Bible says that King David was a man after
God's own heart. When David's adulterous affair with
Bathsheba was exposed, he wasn't afraid of losing his
kingdom. But he was desperate to not lose God's presence. "Create in me a clean heart, O God," he prayed,
"and renew a steadfast spirit within me. *Do not cast me
away from Your presence*, and do not take Your Holy
Spirit from me" (Ps. 51:10–11, emphasis added).

God allows those who are faithful to seek Him
above all else to come before His presence.

Moses was also determined to remain in God's presence. He refused to go into the Promised Land without
the presence of the Lord, even though God had promised

that he and the children of Israel would find blessings there.

> Then the LORD said to Moses, *"Depart and go up from here,* you and the people whom you have brought out of the land of Egypt, to the land of which I swore to Abraham, Isaac, and Jacob, saying, 'To your descendants I will give it.' *And I will send My Angel before you, and I will drive out the Canaanite and the Amorite and the Hittite and the Perizzite and the Hivite and the Jebusite. Go up to a land flowing with milk and honey; for I will not go up in your midst, lest I consume you on the way, for you are a stiff-necked people."*
>
> —EXODUS 33:1–3, emphasis added

But Moses refused to move forward without God's presence. We read in Exodus 33:15:

> Then he said to Him, "If Your Presence does not go with us, do not bring us up from here."

Instead of going on his own, Moses prayed,

> Now therefore…if I have found grace in Your sight, show me now Your way, that I may know You and that I may find grace in Your sight.
>
> —EXODUS 33:13

Show me now Your way—may that be our prayer today! We should never be content to live without God's presence. We should chase after it with all our might. But it will do no good for us to run after God's presence without understanding that there is a right way to come before Him. There is a spiritual protocol. If we discover the principles of this protocol, we will be able to go before the throne room presence of God.

We can learn how to access the secret place by understanding the pattern of the tabernacle. God reveals through the tabernacle seven steps that will take us into a place where we will experience the glory of God. These steps are really seven revelations we must enter into and pass through in order to reach the place called grace.

These seven revelations are made known at seven key locations in the tabernacle. Over the next few chapters we are going to uncover the incredible truths found at each of these locations and learn how they can take us closer to the manifested glory of God. These seven locations are:

1. The gate
2. The brazen altar
3. The brazen laver
4. The altar of incense
5. The golden candlestick
6. The table of showbread
7. The holy of holies

Step by step we will draw closer to God.

Enter His Gates With Thanksgiving

Psalm 100:4 says, "Enter into His gates with thanksgiving, and into His courts with praise. Be thankful to Him, and bless His name." To rightly approach the throne of God, we must first come to Him with thanksgiving in our hearts and our mouths. Many people come to God in prayer with complaints or a spiritual gimme list—"Lord, gimme this, gimme that, and gimme some more."

The Word teaches us to enter His gates with thanksgiving. This means the process of entering God's presence must begin with a grateful heart, not a laundry list of wants. We are reminded throughout Scripture of the need to have a thankful heart before God:

> *Giving thanks always for all things* to God the Father in the name of our Lord Jesus Christ.
> —EPHESIANS 5:20,
> emphasis added

> Be anxious for nothing, but in everything by prayer and supplication, *with thanksgiving,* let your requests be made known to God.
> —PHILIPPIANS 4:6,
> emphasis added

> *Therefore I will give thanks unto thee, O LORD,* among the heathen, and I will sing praises unto thy name.
> —2 SAMUEL 22:50, KJV,
> emphasis added

> *Surely the righteous shall give thanks to Your name;* the upright shall dwell in Your presence.
> —PSALM 140:13,
> emphasis added

> *In every thing give thanks: for this is the will of God*
> in Christ Jesus concerning you.
> —1 Thessalonians 5:18, kjv,
> emphasis added

We must enter His gates with thanksgiving. Everything God does, He does for a divine purpose. True thanksgiving or gratefulness engages several attributes that God is drawn toward. It expresses humility by acknowledging God as our source. When we are thankful, we are acknowledging the kindness and generosity of someone else. People who feel they deserve something are rarely grateful when they receive it.

I knew a young minister who believed God had called him into full-time ministry, so he quit his job and decided to live by "faith." A few days later his roommates decided to pay his share of the rent and food to show their support for his calling. This was a great sacrifice for them since none of them made much money.

Of course, this young minister said thank you because that is what we are taught to do. But that didn't mean he was truly thankful. Deep in his heart he had the idea that since he was "doing the work of the Lord," he really deserved to be taken care of by his brothers in the Lord.

> People who feel they deserve something are rarely grateful when they receive it.

This attitude quickly began to surface in small ways. There were six guys living in a three-bedroom apartment. This young minister had the master bedroom and private bathroom all to himself. When he was working, he paid a little toward the rent for the privilege of having his own space in such a crowded apartment. But because most of the time he was living off the other roommates, they suggested that one of the guys share the room with this minister. Well, this young man had a fit. He said he needed his privacy to "pray."

Although his goal was to go into full-time ministry, he was actually doing ministry only a few hours a week. The rest of the time he spent at home. When the roommates suggested he do more of the cleaning around the house, again he refused, saying it wasn't fair. Incident after incident occurred, one small thing after another, until the roommates began to resent the fact that they had ever offered to help.

You see, although this young minister said thank you, he really wasn't grateful in his heart, because he believed he deserved to be taken care of. This is why many who receive aid from either governments or charities often have terrible attitudes. I know this is not the case with everyone receiving assistance. But I have been around food banks and homeless shelters and have seen attitudes that were so arrogant and prideful, it would shock you. I've met people who believed they were entitled to receive aid and had structured their entire lifestyle around benefiting from the generosity of others.

Most people who have attempted to help someone in need have bumped into these kinds of attitudes— ungrateful, unthankful people who often are that way because they feel they are owed our charity. When a child behaves this way, we say that child is spoiled. Material things don't necessarily cause a child to be spoiled. A lack of gratitude does. The spoiled child feels he deserves all the good things he receives and often begins to demand more.

In the church God has many spoiled children who are not truly grateful for the many blessings He has given them and are always lusting for more. This lack of gratitude is expressed many times through complaining. I believe this is why God hates murmuring, because it is a sign of ungratefulness.

I counsel people all the time who say things such as, "I don't understand why God doesn't do this or that for me." Or, "Why am I not healed?" "Why don't I have a job?" "Why am I late on my bills?" Why? Why? Why?

My wife and I went through a very tough financial season several years ago. We had no money and didn't know where any would come from. I felt stress coming upon me, so I decided to focus on the things I was grateful for. I would wake up every morning and say, "Today I am OK. Thank You, Lord, for Your daily provisions." I was broke, but I still had food, shelter, and clothing. I had much to be grateful for.

Through this season I became filled with a deep joy and peace. It was one of the greatest times in my Christian walk. A joy unspeakable and a peace that passed all understanding flooded my life. That financially tough season ended, but the lesson remained. I learned how to be thankful in *all* things.

Humility is expressed when we are truly thankful for what we have received. When we do this, we are saying to God, "The only thing I deserve is an eternity in hell, yet You have given me all this love and kindness. Even through my hard times You are there. Even when I fall

You are there. Thank You, Lord! Thank You that I have air to breathe, water to drink, clothes on my back, and a roof over my head. Thank You for a voice to praise You with and hands to lift up to You. Thank You for speaking to me even when it is a rebuke. Thank You for allowing me to feel just a little bit of Your presence. Thank You Lord—thank You!"

Those words of thanksgiving you just read were written through tears because as I was writing, God demonstrated this truth about thanksgiving to me in a most amazing way. As I was writing, my oldest son, who was thirteen, came into my office. It was late, and he was supposed to be in bed. But he came into my office because he said he had been thinking.

We have a little joke in my family that whenever he starts thinking, it costs me money. So I smiled, and he immediately said, "It won't cost you anything." I laughed and said, "Oh, are you going to give me money?" He said, "Yes." Then he pulled his hand from behind his back, and I saw that it was filled with bills.

There was a total of twenty-five dollars. He said, "I want you to have this. It is half of my birthday money. I am going to give the other half to God." I sat there still, not knowing what to say. I was trying to figure out a way to give the money back to him when he said, "And no, you can't give it back to me. I wanted to give this to you because you do so much for me."

I was trying to hold back a flood of tears as I hugged and thanked him. I was so touched by his act of thanksgiving that I went into the other room after he returned to bed and cried. The only thing I wanted to do was give him something. I just wanted to run out to the store and buy him the biggest gift I could find.

As I sat there in tears, the Lord spoke to me and said, "This is how I feel every time My people express their gratefulness to Me." The words "Oh the joy that floods my soul" came to my mind, and I thought to myself, "If this is how God feels when we are grateful, those with a thankful heart are going to get overwhelmed with blessings." I felt overwhelmed by God's joy and love. It was intense to say the least.

My son's gift may not have been much in light of all it takes to maintain our home, but it cost him something. Twenty-five dollars for a thirteen-year-old is a lot of money. That is why it meant so much to me.

I pray God allows you to experience His response to our thanksgiving. When we touch His heart with our gratitude, He wants to open the floodgates of heaven and pour out blessings for us. He rushes to us and covers us in His amazing love.

Faith Is Activated Through Thanksgiving

Thanksgiving is recognizing and acknowledging God for who He is and all He does. Thanksgiving also causes us to focus our hearts and minds on God. This focusing and acknowledging of God begins to activate faith, and faith attracts God.

When you were reading my words of thanksgiving to God, I know faith began to bubble up inside some of you. So express your own heart to God. Just try it. Put the book down and spend a few minutes thanking God and watch what happens.

All of a sudden faith will be activated. You will begin

to remember who God is and what He has done for you. This remembrance is what activates your faith. You remember how God has brought you through in the past, and that inspires you to believe He will do it again. Paul reminded himself of God's faithfulness when he was facing death.

> Indeed, we felt within ourselves that we had received the [very] sentence of death, but that was to keep us from trusting in and depending on ourselves instead of on God Who raises the dead. *[For it is He] Who rescued and saved us from such a perilous death, and He will still rescue and save us; in and on Him we have set our hope (our joyful and confident expectation) that He will again deliver us [from danger and destruction and draw us to Himself].*
> —2 CORINTHIANS 1:9–10, AMP,
> emphasis added

Paul knew that because God had delivered him in the past, God would continue to deliver him. Through this remembrance, fresh faith and confidence in God was stirred up. Thanksgiving causes us to remember the goodness of God. This is what the Last Supper was all about. Look at what Jesus did and said:

> For I received from the Lord that which I also delivered to you: that the Lord Jesus on the same night in which He was betrayed *took bread; and when He had given thanks*, He broke it and said,

"Take, eat; this is My body which is broken for you;
do this in remembrance of Me."

—1 CORINTHIANS 11:23–24,
emphasis added

Although there are many deep truths about Communion, one of them is the power of remembrance. We gather together to thank God and remember the Lord Jesus.

Therefore do not be unwise, but understand what the will of the Lord is. And do not be drunk with wine, in which is dissipation; but be filled with the Spirit, speaking to one another in psalms and hymns and spiritual songs, singing and making melody in your heart to the Lord, giving thanks always for all things to God the Father in the name of our Lord Jesus Christ.

—EPHESIANS 5:17–20

Enter His Courts With Praise

Throughout this chapter we have focused on the gate of the tabernacle, the first point of revelation about the proper way to enter into the throne room of God. As we saw in Psalm 100:4, we are not only to enter His gates with thanksgiving, we are also to "enter…His courts with praise. Be thankful to Him, and bless His name."

Again there are many great books and teachings on the subject of praise, and I want to avoid repeating what others have taught so well. But I want to highlight a few keys points that I feel are often lacking in people's understanding of the power and function of praise.

In the church we usually hear the term *praise* in

combination with worship. We have praise and worship services, seminars, concerts, and so on. I have heard many people try to explain the difference between praise and worship. Some say praise is the fast songs, and worship is the slow songs. Others say praise is when we sing about God, and worship is when we sing to God. Still others say praise is when we rejoice, and worship is when we take time to be intimate with God.

All of these explanations are technically wrong. Although I don't believe it's worth getting into debates about the definition of praise and worship, if we want to enter His inner court, we must understand what it means to enter with praise.

> Praise is worship physically expressed.

In the Old Testament there are many words that are translated *praise*. These words cover a wide range of expressions—signing, shouting, raising hands, adoration, singing hymns, and more. We are also instructed to praise God with the trumpet, harp, cymbals, dance, clapping hands, and on and on (Ps. 150). These are all *physical expressions.*

The word that is typically translated to express worship is *shachah.* It means to bow down, humbly pay reverence, and lie prostrate. It speaks to the condition of a heart—a heart of worship has humbled itself in the sight of God and lifts Him up. Praise encompasses all the *physical expressions* of a surrendered, yielded, humble heart before God. In short, praise is worship physically expressed.

There is no true praise without a heart that is humble before God. That is why many of our churches are filled with great music programs but their congregations never enter the courts of the presence of the Lord. The worship teams may sing and play with excellence, but if they don't start with surrendered, humble hearts that desire to exalt God, they will not gain access to the inner courts of God's presence. They will go only as far as unbelievers are allowed to go, even though God has invited them to come further.

We cannot truly praise God without a heart of worship. Neither our private nor our corporate times of praise and worship were meant to be Christian sing-alongs. They were never intended to entertain people or simply prepare the atmosphere for the preaching of the Word. Praise is worship physically expressed, and its aim is to glorify and magnify God, who alone is worthy.

Chapter 12

UNDER THE BLOOD

AFTER WE ENTER His gates with thanksgiving and His courts with praise, we come to the next place of revelation about how to properly enter the throne room of God. That place is the brazen altar. This is where the blood sacrifices would take place in the Old Testament tabernacle. This is where atonement for sins was made. We enter His gates with thanksgiving. We enter His courts with praise. Then we must come under the blood.

> And according to the law almost all things are purified with blood, and without shedding of blood there is no remission.
> —HEBREWS 9:22

> For the life of the flesh is in the blood, and I have given it to you upon the altar to make atonement for your souls; for it is the blood that makes atonement for the soul.
> —LEVITICUS 17:11

No one was allowed to go any farther into the temple without the shedding of blood. Those who proceed toward the manifested presence of God must be justified, or made holy, by the blood of Christ's sacrifice on the cross.

There is power in the blood—the power to forgive and the power to purify. God is holy, and He demands that those who come before Him be holy. Only a holy vessel can stand before the presence of a holy God. When Adam and Eve sinned, God had to drive them from His presence. After that point only with the shed blood of the appropriate sacrifice could anyone enter His presence.

When man sinned, he rejected God's legal authority and was separated from God. God is a God of perfect justice. His Word declares that the "wages of sin is death" (Rom. 6:23). In order for the price of sin to be paid, man had to die. Death is not a state where we cease to exist. Quite the contrary! Death is worse than ceasing to exist. Death is eternal separation from God.

Death, as God calls it, is an eternity devoid of God and His influence; thus everything that is not of God will thrive and permeate in death forever. True believers never really die in the traditional sense; they just change addresses. They spend eternity with the Father.

Death Is a Place of Eternal Torment

The Scriptures give us descriptions of an eternal existence without God. In the Gospel of Luke Jesus tells a parable about a sick beggar named Lazarus who lay outside the gate of a rich man. The wealthy man refused to help Lazarus. He ignored Lazarus's cries for crumbs and left him so destitute dogs licked his sores. Then Lazarus died, and he was carried to a place Scripture calls Abraham's bosom. In time the rich man also died, but he met a different fate.

> Then he cried and said, "Father Abraham, have mercy on me, and send Lazarus, that he may dip the tip of his finger in water and cool my tongue; for I am tormented in this flame."
>
> —LUKE 16:24

Death is a place of torment and flames. We see in the Book of Revelation that death and hell will one day be cast into the lake of fire along with those whose names were not found in the Book of Life.

> And the devil that deceived them was cast into the lake of fire and brimstone, where the beast and the false prophet are, *and shall be tormented day and night for ever and ever.* And I saw a great white throne, and him that sat on it, from whose face the earth and the heaven fled away; and there was found no place for them. And I saw the dead, small and great, stand before God; and the books were opened: and another book was opened, which is the book of life: and the dead were judged out of those things which were written in the books, according to their works. And the sea gave up the dead which were in it; and death and hell delivered up the dead which were in them: and they were judged every man according to their works. *And death and hell were cast into the lake of fire. This is the second death. And whosoever was not*

> *found written in the book of life was cast into the lake of fire.*
>
> —REVELATION 20:10–15, KJV,
> emphasis added

The Word of God is clear: the wages of sin is this death—eternal, tormenting, fire-and-brimstone death. The wages of sin must be paid in order for justice to be met. Jesus paid this price for us. He not only suffered and was crucified on the cross here on earth, but He also experienced the wrath of heaven poured out upon Him as He was tormented in hell. Ephesians 4 says, "Now this, 'He ascended'—what does it mean but that *He also first descended into the lower parts of the earth*? He who descended is also the One who ascended far above all the heavens, that He might fill all things" (vv. 9–10, emphasis added).

When the price for our sin was paid in full, God sent the Holy Spirit to raise Jesus from the dead. Paul wrote: "But if *the Spirit of Him who raised Jesus from the dead* dwells in you, He who raised Christ from the dead will also give life to your mortal bodies through His Spirit who dwells in you" (Rom. 8:11, emphasis added).

Jesus shed His blood and died so we wouldn't have to. If you want to enter the holy of holies, you must come under the blood. You must come into a deep understanding of the work Christ completed on the cross. You must know that it is not your righteousness or personal holiness that gives you access to the glory of God. It is only the blood of Christ. Only He could pay the price for sin.

Jesus suffered the torment of all the sins of all

mankind so you and I would never have to experience the separation from God that is death. In so doing, Jesus transferred to us His righteousness, His equity of character with God. Second Corinthians 5:21 says, "For He made Him who knew no sin to be sin for us, that we might become the righteousness of God in Him."

The brazen altar reveals two requirements for entering into the throne room of God. First, as we have discussed, we must come under the blood by accepting Jesus's sacrifice on the cross. We do this by repenting of our sins and surrendering our lives to God's authority, because the essence of sin is the rejection of God's legal right of authority over our lives. When we give God the legal right of authority over our lives, the transfer of our sin to Christ and then His righteousness to us is complete. At that point we stand blameless before God.

> It is not your righteousness or personal holiness that gives you access to the glory of God. It is only the blood of Christ.

The second thing that must happen at the brazen altar is we must walk in the revelation of the finished work of the cross. I could spend several chapters on this, but I will save that for another book. For now, just put this in your spirit: until you realize that the blood of Christ is the only thing that is sufficient to cleanse you from sin, you will never approach God with true humility. Until you realize that only the blood and not your works can atone for your sins, you will never truly be able to move close to the throne of God. And if you don't know that your sins are under the blood, as you approach His glory you will be filled with such insecurity and inferiority that you will shrink away. Condemnation would control you and drive you from God's presence.

Hebrews 4:16 says we are to *"come boldly to the throne of grace,* that we may obtain mercy and find grace to help in time of need" (emphasis added). And then Hebrews 10:19 says we are to have *"boldness to enter the Holiest by the blood of Jesus"* (emphasis added). We are to come to God boldly, and we can do that only by the blood of Jesus. The boldness, confidence, or *faith* we need to go before God's throne comes only through the revelation of the finished work of the cross.

Through the cross we have been reconciled to God and presented blameless and above reproach in His sight. The Scriptures say:

> For it pleased the Father that in Him all the fullness should dwell, and by Him *to reconcile all things to Himself,* by Him, whether things on earth or things in heaven, *having made peace through the blood of His cross.*
>
> And you, who once were alienated and enemies in your mind by wicked works, yet now He has reconciled in the body of His flesh through death, to present you holy, and blameless, and above reproach in His sight—if indeed you continue in the faith, grounded and steadfast, and are not moved away from the hope of the gospel which you heard.
>
> —Colossians 1:19–23,
> emphasis added

How do you walk in the revelation of the finished work? When you come daily before Him, meditate on what Christ did for you on the cross. Let God give you a fresh, daily revelation of the completeness of Christ's sacrifice.

The Brazen Laver

The next place we come to on our journey to the place called grace is the brazen laver. This was a stand with two bowls of water, one to wash the feet and one to cleanse the hands. Although we are positionally pure before God at the brazen altar, Scripture also tells us that we need daily cleansing from the pollution of the previous day.

The brazen laver speaks to us of daily repentance. Many people have thought all they needed to do was repent once when they accepted Christ. But repentance was never supposed to be a one-time event. It should be a lifestyle.

We need to repent daily for two reasons. First, we need to repent of the sins we still commit, whether sins of omission or commission. In other words, we need to repent of both the sins we realize we committed and the ones we aren't aware of.

The second reason for daily repentance is so that we will live a life of brokenness before God. Not long ago I watched the dedication of a huge new sanctuary on television. Although I was rejoicing for the body of Christ to have such a nice facility to use for His kingdom work, I found several statements that were repeatedly made disturbing.

This church seemed bent on saying that they would

never judge anyone. They said they would never tell anyone they were going to hell or that they were a sinner. They would only tell people of the goodness of heaven.

Again and again the leaders said this church was a place of inclusion, a place where people would never feel condemned or judged. One of the attendees said that every time he comes to this church he feels better and better about himself.

These statements may seem fine and good, but they are completely unscriptural. Why are we in the church today so bent on avoiding conviction, pain, and brokenness? What we call condemnation and judgment many times is simply holy conviction.

Preachers don't want to make people uncomfortable. We want them to feel good about themselves. We don't want people in our services to weep over their sin or cry out to God for mercy because of the wickedness in their hearts. We want people to always feel "uplifted" and "positive."

That is not what the church should look like. A prophetic image of the end-time church is found in the Book of Joel.

> *Blow the trumpet in Zion,*
> And sound an alarm in My holy mountain!
> Let all the inhabitants of the land tremble;
> *For the day of the Lord is coming,*
> *For it is at hand:*
> A day of darkness and gloominess,
> A day of clouds and thick darkness…
>
> "Now, therefore," says the LORD,
> *"Turn to Me with all your heart,*

With fasting, with weeping, and with mourning."
So rend your heart, and not your garments;
Return to the LORD your God,
For He is gracious and merciful,
Slow to anger, and of great kindness;
And He relents from doing harm…
Let the priests, who minister to the LORD,
Weep between the porch and the altar;
Let them say, "Spare Your people, O LORD,
And do not give Your heritage to reproach,
That the nations should rule over them.
Why should they say among the peoples,
'Where is their God?'"

Then the Lord will be zealous for His land,
And pity His people.
The LORD will answer and say to His people,
"Behold, I will send you grain and new wine and
oil,
And you will be satisfied by them;
I will no longer make you a reproach among the
nations.
— JOEL 2:1–2, 12–13, 17–19,
emphasis added

So often we want to avoid feeling pain and sorrow, but look at what the Scriptures tell us:

For even if I made you sorry with my letter, I do not regret it; though I did regret it. For I perceive that the same epistle made you sorry, though only for a while. Now I rejoice, not that you were made sorry, *but that your sorrow led to repentance.* For you were made sorry in a godly manner, that you might suffer loss from us in nothing. *For godly sorrow produces repentance leading to salvation,* not to be regretted; but the sorrow of the world produces death. For observe this very thing, that you sorrowed in a godly manner: *What diligence it produced in you,* what clearing of yourselves, what indignation, what fear, what vehement desire, what zeal, what vindication! In all things you proved yourselves to be clear in this matter. Therefore, although I wrote to you, I did not do it for the sake of him who had done the wrong, nor for the sake of him who suffered wrong, but that our care for you in the sight of God might appear to you. Therefore we have been comforted in your comfort. And we rejoiced exceedingly more for the joy of Titus, because his spirit has been refreshed by you all.

—2 Corinthians 7:8–13,
emphasis added

The Lord is near to those who have a broken heart, and saves such as have a contrite spirit.

—Psalm 34:18,
emphasis added

The sacrifices of God are a broken spirit: a broken and a contrite heart, O God, thou wilt not despise.

—Psalm 51:17, kjv,
emphasis added

For thus says the High and Lofty One
Who inhabits eternity, whose name is Holy:
"I dwell in the high and holy place,
With him who has a contrite and humble spirit."

—Isaiah 57:15,
emphasis added

The Word goes on and on. Brokenness is something God loves and that He requires of those who will dwell with Him in the holy place. Oh, you may be able to make it to heaven by trusting in the saving blood of Christ, but if you want to get to the holy of holies, the place called grace, you must come by way of brokenness and repentance.

The person who stands at the door of the holy place is one whose life is marked by continual repentance, brokenness, and a heart that seeks after God. This brokenness and repentance comes by the Word. We are washed by the water of the Word—the Word that comes and convicts us, producing in us a godly sorrow that will lead us to repentance. When we respond through repentance to His Word, then we are cleansed. First John 1:9 says, "If we confess our sins, He is faithful and just to *forgive us* our *sins and to cleanse us* from all unrighteousness" (emphasis added).

> Brokenness is something God loves and that He requires of those who will dwell with Him in the holy place.

The brazen laver is the place of daily repentance. We enter His gates with thanksgiving and His courts with praise. We must come under the blood and then to the place of brokenness and daily repentance. Only then will we be ready to enter the first of the two chambers of the temple.

Chapter 13

THE HOLY PLACE

THE HOLY PLACE was approximately 15 feet wide, 15 feet high, and 30 feet long. The walls were made with wood that was overlaid with gold.[1] The sense of God in this place must have been awesome. Just a few feet from the holy place was the visible glory of God. It is in the holy place that prayers were offered up. There were three items in this room: the table of showbread, the altar of incense, and the golden candlestick, which was the only source of light. In this chapter we will look at each of these three items.

The Altar of Incense

The priest would burn incense upon this altar, and the smoke would rise up and fill the temple.

> Then another angel, having a golden censer, came and stood at the altar. He was given much incense, that he should offer it with the prayers of all the saints upon the golden altar which was before the throne. And the smoke of the incense, with the

prayers of the saints, ascended before God from the angel's hand.

—REVELATION 8:3–4

The altar of incense is the place of intercession. This is the place where prayers are made and answered. For too long the church has struggled with unanswered prayers. I believe that is because we have failed to learn a powerful truth revealed through this altar.

There is a proper place and way to pray. In our sloppy, irreverent Western Christianity, we have treated God as a buddy and a spiritual Santa Claus. We want God to be at our every beck and call. We want Him to give us whatever we want without regard to what He requires of us.

There is a proper way to approach royalty, and there is a proper way to approach God before we make our requests. This truth is seen throughout the Scriptures. Jesus said in the Gospel of Matthew:

> And when you pray, *you shall not be like the hypocrites.* For they love to pray standing in the synagogues and on the corners of the streets, that they may be seen by men. Assuredly, I say to you, they have their reward. But you, when you pray, go into your room, and when you have shut your door, *pray to your Father who is in the secret place*; and your Father who sees in secret will reward you openly. And when you pray, do not use vain repetitions as the heathen do. For they think that they will be heard for their many words.
>
> Therefore do not be like them. For your Father

knows the things you have need of before you ask Him. In this manner, therefore, pray:

Our Father in heaven,
Hallowed be Your name. [Enter His Gates with
    thanksgiving, His courts with praise.]
Your kingdom come. [This is the brazen altar,
    coming under the authority of Christ.]
Your will be done
On earth as it is in heaven. [The brazen laver, the
    place of daily repentance.]

—MATTHEW 6:5–10,
emphasis added

At this point we are ready to pray for our needs. Jesus says we should now pray:

Give us this day our daily bread.
And forgive us our debts,
As we forgive our debtors.
And do not lead us into temptation,
But deliver us from the evil one.
For Yours is the kingdom and the power and the
    glory forever. Amen.

—MATTHEW 6:11–13

After we have entered His gates with thanksgiving and His courts with praise, after we have come under the blood and repented of our sins, then we are in a proper spiritual position to pray as we ought. Once we are here in the holy place, cleansed afresh by the blood of Jesus, our consciences washed clean, we can truly pray with faith.

Hebrews 10:22 says, "Let us draw near with a true

heart in full assurance of faith, having our hearts sprinkled from an evil conscience and our bodies washed with pure water." And the apostle Paul wrote, "I thank God, *whom I serve with a pure conscience,* as my forefathers did, *as without ceasing I remember you in my prayers night and day*" (2 Tim. 1:3, emphasis added).

> There is a proper way to approach royalty, and there is a proper way to approach God before we make our requests.

Not only do we need to come before God properly before we intercede in order to see the level of prayers answered that God has promised, but we must do so in the right way to avoid judgment. Yes, I said to avoid judgment. Judgment can be what we perceive as punishment, but the greatest judgment is when God will no longer give us access to Himself. Look at the following verses.

> Let him turn away from evil and do good; let him seek peace and pursue it. For the eyes of the LORD are on the righteous, and His ears are open to their prayers; *but the face of the Lord is against those who do evil.*
> —1 PETER 3:11–12, emphasis added

> One who turns away his ear from hearing the law, *even his prayer is an abomination.*
> —PROVERBS 28:9, emphasis added

Set a wicked man over him, and let an accuser stand at his right hand. When he is judged, let him be found guilty, *and let his prayer become sin.*

—PSALM 109:6–7,
emphasis added

Then *they will cry to the Lord,* but *He will not hear them; He will even hide His face from them at that time, because they have been evil in their deeds.*

—MICAH 3:4,
emphasis added

Let us search out and examine our ways, and turn back to the LORD; let us lift our hearts and hands to God in heaven. We have transgressed and rebelled; *You have not pardoned. You have covered Yourself with anger and pursued us; You have slain and not pitied. You have covered Yourself with a cloud, that prayer should not pass through.*

—LAMENTATIONS 3:40–44,
emphasis added

"Behold, you trust in lying words that cannot profit. Will you steal, murder, commit adultery, swear falsely, burn incense to Baal, and walk after other gods whom you do not know, and then come and stand before Me in this house which is called by My name, and say, 'We are delivered to do all these abominations'? Has this house, which is called by My name, become a den of thieves in your eyes? [That sounds a lot like Matthew 21:13, when Jesus chased the money changers out of the temple.] Behold, I, even I, have seen it," says the LORD. "But go now to My place which was in Shiloh, where I set My name at the first, and see what I did to

it because of the wickedness of My people Israel. And now, because you have done all these works," says the LORD, "and I spoke to you, rising up early and speaking, but you did not hear, and I called you, but you did not answer, *therefore I will do to the house which is called by My name, in which you trust, and to this place which I gave to you and your fathers, as I have done to Shiloh. And I will cast you out of My sight,* as I have cast out all your brethren—the whole posterity of Ephraim.

"Therefore do not pray for this people, nor lift up a cry or prayer for them, nor make intercession to Me; *for I will not hear you.*"

—JEREMIAH 7:8–16,
emphasis added

Your New Moons and your appointed feasts My soul hates; they are a trouble to Me, I am weary of bearing them. When you spread out your hands, I will hide My eyes from you; even though you make many prayers, I will not hear. Your hands are full of blood. Wash yourselves, make yourselves clean; put away the evil of your doings from before My eyes. Cease to do evil.

—ISAIAH 1:14–16

Because I have called and you refused, I have stretched out my hand and no one regarded, because you disdained all my counsel, and would have none of my rebuke, I also will laugh at your calamity; I will mock when your terror comes, when your terror comes like a storm, and your destruction comes like a whirlwind, when distress and anguish come upon you.

Then they will call on me, but I will not answer; they will seek me diligently, but they will not find me. Because they hated knowledge and did not choose the fear of the LORD, they would have none of my counsel and despised my every rebuke. Therefore they shall eat the fruit of their own way, and be filled to the full with their own fancies. For the turning away of the simple will slay them, and the complacency of fools will destroy them; but whoever listens to me will dwell safely, and will be secure, without fear of evil.

—PROVERBS 1:24–33

"Yes, they made their hearts like flint, refusing to hear the law and the words which the LORD of hosts had sent by His Spirit through the former prophets. Thus great wrath came from the LORD of hosts. *Therefore it happened, that just as He proclaimed and they would not hear, so they called out and I would not listen," says the LORD of hosts.*

—ZECHARIAH 7:12–13,
emphasis added

God is a God who must be honored. We must not risk grieving the Holy Spirit by being irreverent and disobedient. The holy place is the place of intercession. We must come before God cleansed freshly by the waters of repentance. Then, as the verses above attest, we can intercede and know that He hears and will answer our prayers.

The psalmist wrote:

Who may ascend into the hill of the LORD?
Or who may stand in His holy place?

He who has clean hands and a pure heart,
Who has not lifted up his soul to an idol,
Nor sworn deceitfully.
He shall receive blessing from the LORD.

—PSALM 24:3–5

The holy place is where God always intended for us to come before Him and make our petitions known. This is where God has promised to answer our prayers. The altar of incense reminds us that if we want our prayers heard and answered, we must come before God cleansed.

We must not risk grieving the Holy Spirit
by being irreverent and disobedient.

The Golden Candlestick

The next thing we see in the holy place is the golden candlestick. This was made from one solid piece of gold that was beaten into shape. It held seven candles that would burn day and night, which is why the golden candlestick speaks to us of the continual fire of the Holy Spirit.

We constantly need to be filled afresh with the Holy Spirit. The candlestick reminds us that we need to yield ourselves to the Spirit of God, so He can lead us the rest of the way to the throne room. As you walk toward the glory, stop here and ask for a fresh filling of the Holy Spirit. Wait on Him, for He will come, and He will fill you.

Just spend time waiting on the Spirit of God. Allow the waves of His presence to wash over you. Let the Holy Spirit fill your mind, soul, and body to the point that God becomes the only thing you are thinking of. Get lost in His presence, for only He can take you into the holy of holies.

It amazes me how many Christians have never spent time with the Holy Spirit just soaking in His presence. This is one of the most awesome and precious privileges that we have as believers. I can't tell you the multitudes of times I have just been quiet before God and felt waves of the Holy Spirit sweep over me, sometimes for hours. This time with the Holy Spirit doesn't just refresh us; it also prepares us to meet with the King.

Before Esther was ever presented to King Ahasuerus, she was soaked in perfumes for a year. By the time she came into the presence of the king, her very being smelled of a glorious fragrance. As we spend time with the Holy Spirit soaking in His presence, we begin to take on the aroma of heaven and become presentable to the King of kings.

The Table of Showbread

On the table of showbread were the unleavened bread and the wine. At this table the priests would come and partake of the bread and wine before the presence of God. Of course, this reminds us of Communion, but it also speaks to us of the revelation of Christ.

As we move toward the manifest glory of God, the place called grace where everything we need is, we need to have a sacred intimacy with Jesus. There is a depth of communion revealed at the table of showbread that is so intimate and personal, you almost dare not share it with anyone else.

In the place of communion I am talking about, you are laid bare before Jesus and engaging with Him spirit to Spirit. Words fail to adequately describe this place of intimacy with God. It is a level of communion in the Spirit that transcends anything you will ever experience in the natural.

> We constantly need to be filled
> afresh with the Holy Spirit.

What a husband and wife experience on the marriage bed pales in comparison to this level of intimacy. There are times when married couples who are deeply in love experience a level of intimacy on the marriage bed that transcends the physical and even the emotional. Many call it a spiritual experience, and it is. But as awesome as that can be, it is only a foreshadowing of what God has made available for us at the table of showbread.

Here is where we learn to romance the King. Early in my Christian walk I learned of this place of intimacy with God. I would go for long walks to my secret place of prayer, where I would love on the Lord and feel Him lavish His love on me.

As I would walk to my prayer place, I would stick my hand out and ask the Lord to hold my hand. I would feel His presence come and stand by my side. I would sing and dance before Him, often for hours. Often I would sit on an old tree stump and scoot over so there would be room for the Lord to sit next to me. We would talk for hours.

Other times I would just sit in awe of Him. The intimacy I felt during these times was deeper than anything I had ever known. God desires for all to come to this place, but so many of His children never do. They never take the time to wait in His presence and experience the love of the Bridegroom for us, His bride.

We enter His gates with thanksgiving and His courts with praise. We come under the blood and go to the place of repentance. Then we intercede at the altar of incense. Being filled again and soaked in the Holy Spirit, we then come to the table of intimate communion with God Himself.

All of this is so awesome you could spend a lifetime seeking the truths and levels of intimacy found in each of these places and never even scratch the surface. But God wants us to go further. He wants us to go to a place called grace where everything we need is. He wants us to stand before His manifested glory in the throne room of heaven.

Chapter 14

GOING BEFORE
THE THRONE

PAST THE THICK curtains that were constantly shrouded in smoke was the holy of holies, where once a year the high priest would go and stand before the visible glory of God. The manifest glory was so brilliant and awesome that the priests had to fill the holy of holies with smoke from the altar of incense thick enough to ensure the high priest would not be consumed by the brightness of God's glory.

This is the manifested glory that God has long waited to reveal to His children. It is the visible representation of all that God is and all that He has. For far too long the church has been focused on everything but the one thing that God has been longing for—and that is to bring His children unto Himself and to fully reveal Himself in all His glory.

Everything God has done and all He continues to do is for this one purpose. He longs to share all that He is and all that He has with you and me. God longs to bring us into the fullness of His glory. We read in Colossians:

I now rejoice in my sufferings for you, and fill up in my flesh what is lacking in the afflictions of Christ, for the sake of His body, which is the church, of which I became a minister according to the stewardship from God which was given to me for you, *to fulfill the word of God, the mystery which has been hidden from ages and from generations,* but now has been revealed to His saints. *To them God willed to make known what are the riches of the glory of this mystery among the Gentiles: which is Christ in you, the hope of glory.* Him we preach, warning every man and teaching every man in all wisdom, *that we may present every man perfect in Christ Jesus. To this end I also labor, striving according to His working which works in me mightily.*

—COLOSSIANS 1:24–29,
emphasis added

Paul was focused on this one purpose—that the manifested glory of God would be revealed to and *in* the saints. This is the way we will truly be brought into Christ's own perfection and be transformed into His image. This was the mystery hidden from the ages: that God was going to place His glory—all that He is and all that He has—inside of mankind.

> For far too long the church has been focused on everything but the one thing that God has been longing for— to bring His children unto Himself.

There is a place called grace. It is the throne of God. This is where we will find all things that pertain to life and godliness. This is where our purpose for life will be discovered. This is the only place where we will actually receive what we need to be what God has called us to be. It is here in the holy of holies, the throne of God, the place called grace, where we will truly be changed into His image.

Again Hebrews 4:16 says, "Let us therefore come boldly to the throne of grace, that we may obtain mercy and find grace to help in time of need." And we read in 1 John 3:2 says, "Beloved, now we are children of God; and it has not yet been revealed what we shall be, but we know that *when He is revealed, we shall be like Him, for we shall see Him as He is*" (emphasis added). *When we see Him, we shall be like Him.*

Although this verse in 1 John refers to the final transformation that will take place at the second coming of Christ, it reveals another truth: the more of Jesus we see, the more we become like Him. The more we go to the throne of grace and behold His glory, the more we will be changed into His image.

> But we all, with unveiled face, beholding as in a mirror the glory of the Lord, are being transformed into the same image from glory to glory, just as by the Spirit of the Lord.
>
> —2 Corinthians 3:18

As we behold Jesus's glory, we are being changed into His image. The word translated "transformed" in this verse comes from the Greek word *metamorphoo*, which means to change into another form or transfigure. It is

197

where we get the English word *metamorphosis.* A metamorphosis is a visible, outward manifestation of an inward change.

When a caterpillar goes through a metamorphosis, he comes out of the cocoon completely changed. The caterpillar ceases to exist because it becomes a totally new creature. The butterfly is not a skinny caterpillar with wings. When the metamorphosis takes place, genes that were hidden inside the caterpillar take over. A new heart, new blood, and a new nervous system develop. The butterfly is a whole new creation. It's ready now, after this metamorphosis, to fulfill its God-given purpose.

> When we see Him, we shall be like Him.

As we behold the glory of God, we are undergoing a metamorphosis. The Bible says we are being made brand-new in Christ. He is not redeeming our old nature. He is totally replacing it with a new nature.

> Therefore, if anyone is in Christ, he is a new creation; old things have passed away; *behold, all things have become new.*
> —2 Corinthians 5:17,
> emphasis added

> *I will give you a new heart and put a new spirit within you;* I will take the heart of stone out of your flesh and give you a heart of flesh. I will put My

Spirit within you and cause you to walk in My statutes, and you will keep My judgments and do them.
—EZEKIEL 36:26–27,
emphasis added

For if we have been united together in the likeness of His death, certainly we also shall be in the likeness of His resurrection, *knowing this, that our old man was crucified with Him*, that the body of sin might be done away with, that we should no longer be slaves of sin.
—ROMANS 6:5–6,
emphasis added

That you *put off,* concerning your former conduct, *the old man* which grows corrupt according to the deceitful lusts, and be renewed in the spirit of your mind, and that you *put on the new man which was created according to God, in true righteousness and holiness.*
—EPHESIANS 4:22–24,
emphasis added

As you can see, we are being totally transformed into a new creation, a new man, built according to the exact image of Jesus. This transformation will not happen outside of the throne room of God. Only as we see Him as He is, only as we behold His glory are we going to be changed into His image. "But we all, with unveiled face, beholding as in a mirror the glory of the Lord, are being transformed into the same [His] image from glory to glory" (2 Cor. 3:18).

God has given us His grace—His favor that gives us access to the power of God for everything we need for life and godliness. He has given us access to Himself. God says to us, "Come—come into My throne room presence. By revelation knowledge I have given to you undeserved access to My glory. It is in My glory that you will find everything you need for life and godliness."

Look at the revelation that comes when you put together Hebrews 4:16 and 10:19, 2 Corinthians 3:18 and 4:7, Romans 8:29, and Colossians 1:26–27:

> Let us therefore come boldly to the throne of grace, that we may obtain mercy and find grace to help in time of need....Brethren, having boldness to enter the Holiest by the blood of Jesus...beholding as in a mirror the glory of the Lord, are being transformed into the same [His] image from glory to glory....But we have this treasure in earthen vessels, that the excellence of the power may be of God and not of us....For whom He foreknew, He also predestined to be conformed to the image of His Son....The mystery which has been hidden from ages and from generations, but now has been revealed to His saints. To them God willed to make known what are the riches of the glory of this mystery among the Gentiles: which is Christ in you, the hope of glory.

> Only as we see Him as He is, only as we behold His glory are we going to be changed into His image.

God has called us to enter His gates with thanksgiving and His courts with praise, to come under the blood, and to come to a place of daily repentance. We are to enter the holy place, where we offer true intercession and can be filled with the Spirit. God longs for us to commune with Him at the table of showbread. All of this, though, is to bring us to the one place where everything we need is—the throne of grace, the site of the manifested glory of God.

Grace is the favor of God that gives us access to the power of God for everything we need for life and godliness. Grace gives us access to the very glory of God so we can be transformed into the image of Jesus. As 2 Peter 3:18 says, "Grow in the grace and knowledge of our Lord and Savior Jesus Christ. To Him be the glory both now and forever. Amen."

Chapter 15

PRESS IN TO GOD

L ET'S LOOK AGAIN at the passage we have been examining throughout this book:

> Grace and peace be multiplied to you in the knowledge of God and of Jesus our Lord, as His divine power has given to us all things that pertain to life and godliness, through the knowledge of Him who called us by glory and virtue, by which have been given to us exceedingly great and precious promises, that through these you may be partakers of the divine nature, having escaped the corruption that is in the world through lust.
>
> —2 Peter 1:2–4

God has provided everything we need for life and godliness. He longs for us to be the partakers of His divine nature. From the creation of mankind, God's one desire has been to have someone to share Himself with for all eternity.

We have been challenged through this book to shake off many of our old ways of thinking as we have explored many new ways of viewing grace and the work of Christ in our lives. We now have a choice. Are we going to put this book down and say to ourselves, "That was nice" or "Wow what a revelation!" and then do nothing about it?

> God's one desire has been to have someone to share Himself with for all eternity.

Are we going to let the fowl of the air steal the word before it even takes root (Matt. 13:4)? Are we going to lose it the first time we step out and our attempts to walk in this higher level of living don't work out the way we hoped? Are we going to let the test of failure destroy this word we've received from God?

Can we press on through the point of blessing, where this revelation really starts working for us, and not become distracted by the "success" it brings? Do we have the spiritual fortitude to press all the way through to the place where this revelation of God's grace will truly be able to produce a harvest of thirty, sixty, or a hundredfold?

The awesomeness of what God has provided for us through His grace should cause us to fall upon our knees and cry out in worship, for we are not at all worthy of what He has provided for us. We are not worthy of the privilege of coming before Him or of receiving all the things we need for life and godliness.

Grace, God's undeserved favor, has been given to us so that we can have access to Him. He longs for us to be with Him. It is in His manifested presence that mankind can once again eat from the tree of life and have all that we need for life and godliness.

God in these last days has opened the windows of heaven to give us revelation so we can have access to Him. We must press in boldly. We must take on the nature of God revealed in Matthew 11:12: "And from the days of John the Baptist until the present time, the kingdom of heaven has endured violent assault, *and violent men seize it by force* [as a precious prize—*a share in the heavenly kingdom is sought with most ardent zeal and intense exertion*]" (AMP, emphasis added).

We must be unwilling to yield to complacency and lukewarmness. We must take on the nature of the early church and press into God with all of our hearts. We must take time to search the Word and seek His face. As we do, God will draw near to us and pour out the spirit of revelation upon us. This revelation will cause grace to be multiplied in our lives. It will give us the favor to access the power of God for all things we need for life and godliness.

> The awesomeness of what God has provided for us through His grace should cause us to fall upon our knees and cry out in worship.

So let us enter His gates with thanksgiving and His courts with praise. We'll go past the place of the blood through daily repentance. Entering the holy place, where we truly begin to experience intercession, we then become filled once again with His Holy Spirit. Feasting at the table of showbread, we commune with Jesus as we, step by step, pass through the veil into the manifested glory of God.

This is the place God has called us to, and this is the place we should always long to be. Not a place where we cower from sin and believe the Christian life will bring us little more than a ticket out of hell. We must press in to this place called grace, this place of power, where everything we need is.

NOTES

Chapter 5
Revelation Gifts

1. Biblestudytools.com, *Matthew Henry Complete Commentary on the Whole Bible*, "2 Kings 2" http://www
.biblestudytools.com/commentaries/matthew-henry-complete/
2-kings/2.html, emphasis added (accessed June 24, 2013).

Chapter 6
All Things That Pertain to Life

1. Mira Kirshenbaum, *The Emotional Energy Factor* (New York: Delta, 2003); http://www.chestnuthillinstitute.com/books/
eef/excerpt.php (accessed April 9, 2013).

Chapter 8
Setting the Record Straight

1. Brainy Quote, "Billy Sunday Quotes," http://www
.brainyquote.com/quotes/authors/b/billy_sunday.html (accessed May 14, 2013).

2. As quoted in Flo Ellers, *Activating the Angelic* (Shippensburg, PA: Destiny Image Publishers Inc., 2008).

3. Beliefnet.com, "Inspirational Quotes," http://www
.beliefnet.com/Quotes/Evangelical/J/John-Wesley/Give-Me-One
-Hundred-Preachers-Who-Fear-Nothing-But.aspx (accessed May 14, 2013).

4. Charles H. Spurgeon, *All of Grace* (Chicago, IL: Moody Publishers, 2010). Viewed online at Google Books.

5. Blue Letter Bible, "Dictionary and Word Search for *elegchō* (Strong's 1651)," http://www.blueletterbible.org/lang/lexicon/lexicon.cfm?strongs=G1651&t=KJV (accessed May 14, 2013).

6. *Merriam-Webster's Collegiate Dictionary*, 11th edition (Springfield, MA: Merriam-Webster, Inc., 2003), s.v. "repent."

7. Blue Letter Bible. "Dictionary and Word Search for *metanoeō* (Strong's 3340)," http://www.blueletterbible.org/lang/lexicon/lexicon.cfm?strongs=G3340&t=KJV (accessed May 14, 2013).

8. Charles Finney, *Lectures to Professing Christians* (n.p., Milner, 1837). Viewed at Google Books.

Chapter 13
The Holy Place

1. David M. Levy, *The Tabernacle: Shadows of the Messiah: Its Sacrifices, Services, and Priesthood* (Grand Rapids, MI: Kregel Publications, 2003), 18.

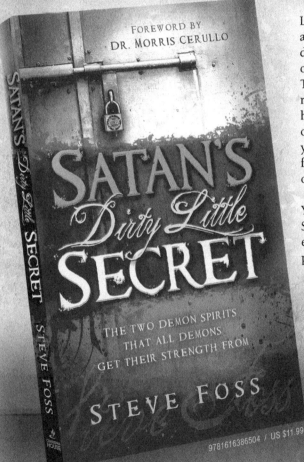

FREE NEWSLETTERS
TO HELP EMPOWER YOUR LIFE

Why subscribe today?

- ❑ **DELIVERED DIRECTLY TO YOU.** All you have to do is open your inbox and read.

- ❑ **EXCLUSIVE CONTENT.** We cover the news overlooked by the mainstream press.

- ❑ **STAY CURRENT.** Find the latest court rulings, revivals, and cultural trends.

- ❑ **UPDATE OTHERS.** Easy to forward to friends and family with the click of your mouse.

CHOOSE THE E-NEWSLETTER THAT INTERESTS YOU MOST:

- • Christian news
- • Daily devotionals
- • Spiritual empowerment
- • And much, much more

SIGN UP AT: **http://freenewsletters.charismamag.com**

8178